EAT, SKI & REPEAT

To Mum — thank you for inspiring my love of good food, supporting every wild adventure, and showing me that the sky is never the limit.

EAT, SKI & REPEAT

BIG SNOW, BOLD FLAVORS
AN ALPINE COOKBOOK

EWA LUBIENSKI

- 7 Why Ski?
- 8 Introduction
- 12 Cooking Above the Clouds
- 13 Feeding the Lodge
- 14 Nutrition for the Slopes
- 15 Behind the Recipes, Beyond the Kitchen
- 18 From Our Kitchen to Yours
- 19 Pick Your Line

21 MOUNTAIN MORNING BAKES

33 FIRST TRACKS BREAKFASTS

45 APRÈS-SKI FIRESIDE APPETIZERS

63 SUMMIT SOUPS

75 SKI LODGE SALADS

87 MAINS TO MELT THE SNOW

105 ON THE SIDE

117 DESSERTS TO END YOUR DAY

141 MOUNTAIN MORSELS: A LITTLE BIT OF EVERYTHING

149 CHILLED AND FILLED: SNOWCAT SANDWICHES

- 155 Appendix
- 156 Well-Being for Skiers
- 158 Snow Science and Fun Facts
- 161 Chasing the Perfect Powder
- 162 The Evolution of Cat Skiing
- 163 Cat Skiing Terminology
- 171 Pantry & produce
- 172 Thank you!
- 174 About the Author

WHY SKI?

Psychologists have tried to explain it, skiers speculate about it, and ordinary people simply shake their heads in dismay. There are no scores or points for skiing—it's about the atmosphere, the grace of movement, and the quiet confidence it brings, better than winning a game. It offers an escape from the noise of everyday life and awakens a deep appreciation for the grandeur of nature. Though it can be physically demanding, no other sport delivers the same sense of fulfillment and awe.

To truly understand why we ski, you must live it. Words fall short. You need to spend the hours, the days, the weeks. You need to meet the people who ski—the individualist, the nonconformist—who are drawn to the mountains. You must witness the breathtaking beauty of snowy peaks and valleys. Skiing is a moment of truth, a personal experience that can't be explained. To understand why we ski, you must become a skier.

INTRODUCTION

Imagine a world where the powder is endless and Mother Nature exists in her rawest form. Moose and mountain caribou roam the backcountry, while bears rest peacefully in their dens, deep in the woods. Elusive wolverines leave their tracks, cryptic clues of their fierce and solitary presence in the wild. Amid this untamed wintery haven, there is a ski lodge—a sanctuary of warmth, hearty meals, and stories shared by the fire, plus a home to a cheeky pine marten, who is always on the prowl for an unattended snack, adding a dash of mischief to the cozy retreat. This rugged wilderness and its curious residents set the stage for unforgettable moments, both on the slopes and around the dinner table.

After a thrilling day of carving through the fluff, return to warmth and hearty home-cooked meals, ready to fuel your next adventure. Here, skiing and good food go hand in hand—the rush of a perfect run with the comfort of a delicious meal. Take your place at the table and prepare for a feast as memorable as the slopes themselves, where nature and flavor collide!

WHERE IT ALL BEGAN

K3 Cat Ski, nestled in the snow-covered Monashee Mountains of British Columbia, started as the ultimate "let's have some fun" project. Founders David and Kris Moore—a father-and-son team from Sicamous—spent their summers running a family-owned forestry business nearby. With a deep bond to the mountains and a shared passion for the outdoors, they turned their love of adventure into something truly special.

Once they got their hands on a snowcat, they took turns behind the wheel, chauffeuring powder-hungry friends into the backcountry. So, what began as a playful off-season escape quickly snowballed into a full-blown passion for sharing unforgettable mountain adventures.

The name K3 goes back to those early days. David and Kris had a little six-person snowcat parked high on the Gorge side of the valley and would snowmobile up to ski with friends. From that perch, they were always staring across at a big, untouched peak they hadn't explored yet.

Back then, most of the mountains in the area didn't even have names. This one was simply known by its location—"the mountain you access from kilometer three on the Gorge Forest Service Road," a logging road deep in the valley. It was a mouthful, but over time, the shorthand stuck. People started calling it "K3," and the name caught on.

As the Gorge side grew more crowded with ski tourers, David and Kris set their sights on that same inviting mountain they'd been eyeing for years. In 2006 they applied for a new tenure there—unrelated to any forestry work—and after eight years of waiting, it finally became official. The once-unnamed mountain that had long lived in their imaginations was now, truly, K3.

The tenure had nothing to do with forestry—it was a separate dream altogether. For the first couple of winters, it was still just about fun: friends, powder, and a snowcat. But by 2008, they figured others might want in. And just like that, K3 Cat Ski officially launched.

* * *

As word spread and demand grew, it was clear that one cat wasn't enough. That's when Rod entered the scene—a fellow snow lover from the early days who saw the potential in K3 and stepped in to help expand the day-skiing operation. With his support, the team grew the fleet to three cats, each rolling out daily with riders eager to explore fresh, untouched terrain.

With their shared passion and vision, David, Kris, and Rod shaped K3 into a world-class cat skiing destination—where the terrain is legendary and the camaraderie runs deep.

To offer guests a more immersive experience, they built South Park Lodge in 2019, a cozy alpine retreat for up to ten guests looking to stay overnight and enjoy back-to-back days in the powder. After several successful seasons, they added a second lodge—Far Side—a mirror image of South Park, welcoming even more skiers into the K3 community.

The spirit of K3 cat skiing was shaped not only by deep powder but by the connections made after the runs were done. In its infancy, when the operation was still small and tight knit, everyone would head back to David and his wife Colleen's home after a day in the mountains. Colleen's home-cooked meals filled the air with warmth, and the dining table became a gathering place—where stories were swapped, laughter flowed, and bonds formed over hearty food and shared stoke.

Colleen's hospitality wasn't just about feeding skiers—it was about creating a sense of belonging. That welcoming energy became the heartbeat of K3.

As the operation grew, David, Kris, and Rod set out to preserve that same feeling. They envisioned a place where guests didn't just ski incredible terrain—they felt truly at home. From arrival to the final meal, every detail reflects that founding spirit of connection, care, and community.

ALTITUDE ADJUSTMENTS

COOKING ABOVE THE CLOUDS

The kitchen at the lodge is a warm, inviting space where I get to be creative, but cooking at high altitude comes with its own set of challenges. Lower air pressure, longer cooking times, and increased evaporation all play a role. For example, at 3,000 meters, water boils at around 194°F (90°C) instead of the usual 212°F (100°C), so food takes longer to cook, especially when boiling or simmering. This can make achieving the right texture for rice and pasta tricky.

The lodge has a propane oven, which can be unpredictable—temperature fluctuations are common, and it's less consistent than an electric oven. To stay on track, I always preheat the oven thoroughly, give it extra time to reach the right temperature, and use an oven thermometer for accuracy. I often set the temperature 5°F to 10°F higher, since propane ovens lose heat quickly when the door opens and baking times tend to be shorter. To prevent uneven cooking, I rotate my baked goods halfway through and check for doneness with a toothpick. Like any oven, there are hot spots, so paying attention to placement and timing ensures everything bakes up perfectly. With a few adjustments, even a temperamental propane oven delivers delicious results.

Baking at high altitude presents its own hurdles. The reduced air pressure causes baked goods to rise more easily, but they can overexpand and collapse. To avoid this, I often adjust recipes by reducing leavening agents like baking powder or baking soda and adding extra flour to strengthen the structure. When baking bread with yeast, I remember that yeast rises faster at higher altitudes, which can result in coarse, uneven textures. To counteract this, I punch down the dough more frequently or let it rise slowly in a cooler space. Adjusting the ratios of liquid and sugar helps preserve moisture and sweetness, leading to more consistent results. I also love incorporating fruit into my baked goods and muffins to balance the dryness and add a flavorful, healthy touch. Since the oven needs to be slightly hotter at altitude, I make my baked goods smaller and cook them faster to ensure they turn out perfectly.

At higher altitudes, liquids evaporate faster due to the lower boiling point, so I add more liquid to recipes and use lids or covered pots for soups and stews to keep things moist. I'm a fan of adding plenty of vegetables to saucy dishes for extra flavor and heartiness. Roasting and grilling may take longer or require lower heat to prevent drying out, but braising and slow cooking work particularly well.

Sugar also behaves differently at high altitudes, becoming more concentrated and causing foods to brown more quickly. To avoid burning, I use a little less sugar and keep a close eye on cooking times. You may also notice that flavors seem a bit muted, so I adjust seasonings and spices to keep my dishes vibrant and delicious. Cooking at higher elevations is all about experimenting and tweaking recipes to discover what works best for you.

SNOW SUPPLY CHAIN

FEEDING THE LODGE

While most marvel at the feasts that appear on our cozy dining table, few consider the journey behind each plate. Getting food to the lodge is no small feat—it's a logistical choreography involving snow-covered roads, delivery vehicles, snowmobiles, and a determined soul sourcing ingredients from valued purveyors. Fresh produce is purchased locally to maintain freshness and minimize delays. Our beer and wine hail from Kelowna, meat and poultry from Salmon Arm, fish from Vernon, and dairy items and nonperishables from Sicamous. Ensuring our produce is sustainably sourced and minimally packaged is a top priority. It keeps things simple for transport and cuts down on the waste we'd have to deal with in our remote location. Kris lives on a charming old blueberry farm in a beautifully renovated farmhouse, surrounded by one hundred thriving blueberry bushes—which means I have the delicious privilege of using homegrown blueberries in countless recipes. These berries are just one example of the many thoughtful, local touches that bring freshness and heart to every dish we serve.

Complicating matters are the unpredictable whims of mountain weather. Transport challenges are constant, as supply trucks must navigate icy, steep, and winding alpine passes. These routes can be treacherous, especially in winter, with black ice, snowdrifts, and blizzards. Snowstorms and avalanches often close roads, particularly Rogers Pass, the critical link between Calgary and Revelstoke. There are two other passes between Calgary and Sicamous, so driving at night can be hazardous due to the precarious conditions. When trucks are delayed, shelves remain empty, and some ingredients simply don't make it to our kitchen. Supply chain disruptions are a part of life up here, so creativity is an essential skill.

After sourcing and purchasing the produce, goods are transported to Sicamous, then reloaded into a four-wheel drive for the eight-mile (thirteen-kilometer) journey up a snow-covered road to a staging area. From there, they're transferred to snowmobiles, covered with a tarp to protect the goods, and driven the final stretch to the lodge. Offloading is always a team effort, and it's not uncommon for the produce to arrive in my kitchen with a light dusting of snow. The unpacking must be quick, as the local pine marten, crows, and ravens are quick to swoop in and help themselves to anything under the tarp if the snowmobile is left unattended.

With limited storage at the lodge, we keep things running smoothly by scheduling deliveries twice a week to make space for fresh goods. While menus are planned, flexibility is key—mountain life demands last-minute improvisation when fresh produce doesn't arrive as expected. Adaptability isn't just a skill here; it's a way of life.

At the lodge, coffee is as essential as fresh snow. We've traded wasteful pods for a high-tech machine that brews barista-quality coffee from freshly ground beans. From bold morning espressos to smooth après-ski lattes, guests gather here to swap trail tips and warm up—rich flavor, no plastic waste, just great coffee that's kinder to the planet.

FUELING THE ADVENTURE

NUTRITION FOR THE SLOPES

Skiing is a full-body, calorie-torching workout that demands serious fuel. Between carving turns, braving the cold, and navigating high-altitude terrain, your body needs the right nutrients to power through the day—and recover for the next.

Start with vitamin D, which plays a big role in keeping bones strong and your immune system in shape—especially when you're out in the cold all day. You'll find it in sunlight (when you can get it), fatty fish, egg yolks, and fortified foods. Vitamin C is your immune system's wingman in chilly weather. Load up on citrus fruits, strawberries, kiwi, bell peppers, or broccoli to help fend off illness and fatigue.

Carbs are your go-to for energy. Complex carbs like oats, whole grains, and brown rice provide steady fuel throughout the day. For quicker bursts—say, mid-morning on the lift—reach for fruit or a bit of honey. Protein steps in for muscle recovery after a day of shredding. Lean meats, eggs, beans, tofu, and yogurt all do the job. And don't forget healthy fats. Avocados, nuts, seeds, and olive oil keep energy levels stable and help your body absorb vitamins A, D, E, and K.

Hydration matters more than you think. Even in cold weather, skiing leads to fluid loss—especially at altitude. Sip water regularly (don't chug!) so your body can keep up. Toss in some electrolytes—sodium, potassium, magnesium—to replace what you're sweating out, even if you don't notice it.

Breakfast sets the tone. Carbs like oats or fruit give you that first energy kick, protein from eggs or yogurt helps you stay full and focused, and healthy fats—chia seeds, avocado, or nut butter—keep you going longer and warmer. Snacking throughout the day is a game-changer. Think trail mix, granola bars, or fruit between runs to keep your energy up and muscles happy. And don't skip lunch—it's your fuel for the afternoon grind.

Once the skis come off, recovery kicks in. Your muscles need protein and carbs—ideally within an hour—to bounce back strong. A smoothie with yogurt, berries, banana, and a little honey hits all the right notes. Keep sipping water or a recovery drink to help your body rehydrate and get ready for another day of mountain magic.

BEHIND THE RECIPES, BEYOND THE KITCHEN

This book began as a chaotic collection of scribbled notes—recipes jotted on Post-it notes, scrawled on the backs of receipts, or hastily written on whatever scrap of paper was within reach. My handwriting was a blur, rushed and often illegible—after all, I was usually racing to get breakfast sorted before jumping into the snowcat for a few runs on the mountain. At times, it looked more like a doctor's prescription pad than anything resembling a cookbook. I'd often have to go back to the original sources—old cookbooks, bookmarked websites—just to make sense of my own measurements.

But over several seasons, these scraps turned into something more. The dishes I cooked were enjoyed by guests and staff alike, and slowly the recipes became part of the lodge's rhythm as certain meals were requested repeatedly. Over time, and often with a glass of wine in hand at the end of a long day, I began to gather and shape the recipes into something more intentional.

That's when the stories began to weave themselves in. I realized this wasn't just a collection of recipes—it reflected a place, and the people who bring it to life. Some dishes are linked to iconic ski runs at K3, others to the mountain guides and lodge staff who've shaped so many of our days. Scattered throughout are anecdotes of the characters who left their mark—some by guests who returned year after year, always asking for the same dish, often asking for the recipe and the secrets behind it.

These recipes come straight from my personal experience—I created each one, inspired both by dishes I've developed myself and by the stories and moments shared with guests and staff over the years. But every dish holds a memory: laughter ringing out around the dinner table, boots lined up to dry in the warm ski room, fleeting moments that grew into lasting friendships.

This book is more than a cookbook. It's a patchwork of food, stories, and the community that forms each winter at the lodge. It's messy, heartfelt, and personal—just like the best meals always are.

FROM OUR KITCHEN TO YOURS

EAT, SKI & REPEAT

This cookbook is your official invite to dig into the hearty, nourishing fare we serve up at the lodge—and maybe impress a few friends along the way. It's filled with everything we've learned about cooking well when you are miles from the nearest grocery store (and maybe running a little low on Wi-Fi).

Inside, you'll find nine lively chapters packed with wholesome recipes, cozy flavors, and plenty of lodge-style charm. While most dishes are built around comfort, balance, and big mountain appetites, a few come with an extra layer of personality—tied to specific runs at K3 or inspired by the stories of our staff and guests. These recipes are sprinkled with anecdotes and memories, making them feel as personal as a fireside chat after a day on the slopes.

This isn't just about food—it's about the spirit that brings people together in the mountains. Every dish is crafted with care, easy to make wherever you are, and full of the kind of comfort that Makes you want to settle in with a second helping (or third—we won't judge). Consider it your taste of mountain life, with a little fun and a few kitchen mishaps along the way.

Start your day with **Mountain Morning Bakes**, a collection of oven-fresh creations made to warm you up and get you going. When it's time to gear up and chase fresh powder, **First Tracks Breakfasts** have your back with hearty, energizing meals designed to power every turn and trail.

After a long day on the mountain, it's time to kick off the evening with **Après-Ski Fireside Appetizers**—satisfying, snackable bites that pair perfectly with a cold drink and a round of mountain stories. And nothing hits the spot like a bowl from **Summit Soups**—the kind of soul-warming comfort that brings everyone back to the table.

Every great dinner starts with something fresh, and **Ski Lodge Salads** are just the thing—crisp, colorful, and packed with bold flavors. Then come the stars of the table: **Mains to Melt the Snow**. These dishes are fun, flavorful, and just the right kind of hearty to satisfy après-ski appetites.

No meal is complete without the perfect accompaniment, and the dishes in **On the Side** are here to round things out—simple, reliable, and designed to shine alongside the mains.

When it's time for something sweet, turn to **Desserts to End Your Day**—a collection of cozy, indulgent treats to wrap up your mountain adventures on a high note. And don't miss **Mountain Morsels**, our stash of irresistible little extras that don't quite fit into a box—but are too good to leave out.

Each recipe in this book has been tested and perfected right here at the lodge. So, grab a fork, pull up a chair, and dig into the delicious rhythm of mountain life.

PICK YOUR LINE

Just like choosing your line on the mountain, every recipe in this book comes with its own kind of ride. Some are mellow groomers, perfect for lazy lodge mornings or après-ski snacks. Others are full send—big flavor, bold moves, and a bit of a challenge. To help you navigate, I've tagged every recipe with a difficulty marker:

🟢 CAT TRACKS
Laid-back laps for cozy comfort
These easygoing recipes are perfect for beginners, busy days, or anyone looking for simple satisfaction with zero stress. Think mellow vibes, minimal prep, and maximum comfort—your culinary groomers.

🟦 ROLLERS
Playful terrain with a little bounce
Step it up a notch with dishes that add a bit more flavor, flair, and finesse. These are your fun, twisty runs—ideal for intermediate cooks ready to carve their way through something tasty.

◆ DROP ZONE
Steep lines, big flavor—send it
You've reached expert terrain. These recipes take some skill and confidence, but the payoff is epic. Whether it's layers of flavor or just a little culinary risk, it's time to drop in and go full send.

For those who are coasting and for those who are charging hard, this book's got a line for every kind of rider. Choose your terrain and dig in!

MOUNTAIN MORNING BAKES

There's nothing quite like waking up deep in the mountains to the smell of something baking in the oven while snow piles up quietly outside. At K3, every morning begins with freshly baked treats—still warm from the oven and set out on the breakfast table alongside the rest of the spread, ready for guests as they wander down to eat. Whatever doesn't vanish by the end of breakfast gets tucked into the cooler, ready to be shared in the cat between powder laps. Here are nine of the most requested and often-repeated recipes from our mornings at the lodge.

PEAR AND PECAN CRUMBLE CAKE

SERVES

10

CAKE

¼ cup (57 g) unsalted butter, at room temperature

½ cup (100 g) packed brown sugar

1 egg

1 tsp. (5 g) vanilla

1 cup (240 ml) unsweetened applesauce

1 + ½ cup (180 g) all-purpose flour

½ tsp. (2 g) baking powder

½ tsp. (2 g) baking soda

1 tsp. (2. 6g) ground cinnamon

¼ tsp. (1.5 g) salt

2 Ripe pears, peeled and diced

STREUSEL TOPPING

½ cup (100 g) packed brown sugar

¼ cup (57 g) unsalted butter, melted

2 tbsp. (15 g) all-purpose flour

¾ cup (90 g) pecans, roughly chopped

This cake is a testament to the art of improvisation at the lodge. It was originally meant to be made with apples, but when a delivery didn't arrive on time, I swapped in ripe pears instead—and never looked back. Pear and Pecan Crumble Cake has since become a beloved breakfast indulgence. This rustic beauty pairs the mellow sweetness of juicy pears with the satisfying crunch of toasted pecans, all crowned with a golden, buttery crumble.

1. Preheat the oven to 350°F (175°C). Grease a 9 x 5-inch (23 x 13 cm) loaf tin or line it with parchment paper, leaving some overhang for easy removal.

2. In a large bowl, cream the butter and brown sugar until light and fluffy—use a hand mixer for ease. Add the egg and vanilla, mixing until everything is smooth and fully blended.

3. Stir in the applesauce until well combined. This step Makes the cake incredibly moist and adds a subtle fruity sweetness.

4. In a separate bowl, whisk together the flour, baking powder, baking soda, cinnamon, and salt. Whisking ensures the leavening agents are evenly distributed for a consistent rise

5. Gradually add the dry ingredients to the wet mixture in batches. Stir gently until just combined

6. Using a spatula, gently fold in the pears. Be careful not to mash them; we want juicy pear chunks in every bite.

7. For the streusel topping, in a medium bowl combine the brown sugar, butter, and flour. Use your fingers or a pastry cutter to mix until it resembles coarse crumbs—small, buttery clumps are key for a crumbly texture. Stir in the pecans to add crunch.

8. Pour the batter into the prepared loaf tin, spreading it out evenly. Sprinkle the streusel topping generously over the top.

9. Bake the cake for 40 to 50 minutes. The cake is ready when a toothpick inserted into the center comes out clean, and your kitchen smells heavenly.

10. Let the cake cool in the tin for 10 minutes before lifting it out using the parchment paper sling. Transfer it to a wire rack to cool completely.

ORANGE PUMPKIN MUFFINS WITH CITRUS GLAZE

MAKES
12 MUFFINS

MUFFINS

⅓ cup (80 ml) coconut oil, at room temperature

½ cup (120 ml) honey

1 cup (240 ml) pumpkin puree

2 eggs

⅓ cup (80 ml) freshly squeezed orange juice

Zest from 2 large oranges

1 tsp. (5 g) vanilla

2 cups (250 g) all-purpose flour

1 tsp. (4 g) baking soda

2 tsp. (10 g) ground cinnamon

½ tsp. (2.5g) ground ginger

¼ tsp. (1. 5g) salt

½ cup (80 g) golden raisins

GLAZE

¾ cup (90 g) powdered sugar, sifted

1–2 tbsp. (15–30 ml) freshly squeezed lemon juice (adjust for desired consistency)

1 tsp. (2 g) lemon zest

Pumpkin is my go-to comfort ingredient once the temperatures drop—it's cozy, versatile, and always finds a spot on the winter menu at the lodge, whether in soups, stews, or a batch of spiced muffins. These orange pumpkin muffins are a personal favorite for chilly mornings. Naturally sweetened with honey and made with coconut oil instead of seed oils, they feel just a little bit wholesome while still tasting like a treat.

1. Preheat the oven to 350°F (175°C). Line a 12-cup muffin tin with paper cups or grease generously with coconut oil to ensure easy release.

2. In a large bowl, blend the coconut oil and honey until well combined. Then stir in the pumpkin puree, eggs, orange juice, zest, and vanilla extract. Whisk until everything is smooth and creamy. The pumpkin adds moisture and flavor that's perfect for fall!

3. In a separate bowl, whisk the flour, baking soda, cinnamon, ginger, and salt. This step ensures the spices are evenly distributed.

4. Gradually add the dry ingredients to the wet mixture, stirring until just combined. No overmixing—we want these muffins light and fluffy! Gently fold in the golden raisins for those sweet, chewy bites.

5. Divide the batter evenly among the prepared muffin cups, filling each about three-quarters full.

6. Bake for about 15 to 20 minutes. The muffins are ready when a toothpick inserted in the middle comes out clean and the tops are a gorgeous golden brown. Your kitchen will smell like heaven!

7. While the muffins bake, prepare the glaze. Combine the powdered sugar, lemon juice and zest. Stir until smooth and drizzle ready.

8. Allow the muffins to cool in the pan for about 10 minutes, then transfer to a wire rack to cool completely. Drizzle the glaze over the muffins for a sweet, citrus finish. It adds a delightful tang that complements the pumpkin perfectly.

BLUEBERRY BUCKLE BREAD

SERVES 10

BREAD

¾ cup (150 g) granulated sugar

¼ cup (57 g) unsalted butter, at room temperature

1 egg

2 cups (250 g) all-purpose flour

2 tsp. (8 g) baking powder

¼ tsp. (1.5 g) salt

½ cup (120 ml) milk

2 ripe bananas, mashed

1 tsp. (2 g) lime zest

2 cups (280 g) blueberries (fresh is best, but frozen works too)

STREUSEL TOPPING

⅓ cup (65 g) brown sugar

½ cup (62 g) all-purpose flour

1 tsp. (2.6 g) ground cinnamon

¼ cup (57 g) unsalted butter, cold and cut into small pieces

¼ cup (30 g) walnuts, finely chopped

Get ready for a flavor-packed treat! Juicy blueberries burst with every bite, while ripe bananas add natural sweetness—so there's no need for much added sugar. We like to keep things on the healthier side! At K3, we make it extra special with blueberries picked straight from Kris's Garden. A buttery, crumbly streusel tops this delight, adding the perfect crunch with a hint of cinnamon. Each slice is a perfect balance of textures and flavors.

1. Preheat the oven to 350°F (175°C). Grease a 9 x 5-inch (23 x 13 cm) loaf pan or line it with parchment paper for easy removal.

2. In a large bowl, combine the sugar, butter, and egg. Grab your hand mixer and beat until the mixture is light and fluffy; this will create a lovely texture for your cake.

3. In a separate bowl, whisk the flour, baking powder, and salt. This helps ensure that the leavening agent is evenly distributed.

4. Fold the flour mixture into the butter mixture in two batches, alternating with the milk, and give the batter a quick beat after each addition to incorporate everything nicely, being careful not to overmix the batter.

5. In a separate bowl, mash the bananas with a fork until smooth, like applesauce. The riper the bananas, the sweeter and more flavorful your cake will be! Gently fold the bananas into the batter until just combined, then add the lime zest. This elevates the flavor.

6. Gently fold in the blueberries, taking care not to overmix so the berries stay intact. This will give your cake those delicious bursts of blueberry in every bite. Pour the mixture into your prepared pan and set it aside.

7. Make the streusel topping. In a small bowl, combine the brown sugar, flour, cinnamon, and butter. Use your hands to work the butter into the dry ingredients until it forms a crumbly, streusel-like texture.

8. Transfer the batter to the prepared loaf pan, sprinkle the topping evenly over the cake batter, and bake for 30 to 40 minutes, or until a toothpick inserted into the center of the cake comes out clean. Enjoy the delightful aroma as it bakes!

9. Let the cake cool for a few minutes before removing it from the pan. Slice and serve.

RASPBERRY STREUSEL TOP MUFFINS

MAKES
12 MUFFINS

STREUSEL TOPPING

1 cup (125 g) all-purpose flour

¾ cup (150 g) brown sugar

⅓ cup (76 g) cold unsalted butter, cut into small cubes

MUFFINS

1 + ¾ cups (210 g) all-purpose flour

1 tsp. (4 g) baking powder

1 tsp. (4 g) baking soda

1 tsp. (2.6 g) ground cinnamon

¼ tsp. (1.5 g) salt

¾ cup (150 g) brown sugar

2 eggs

1 banana, mashed

½ cup (113 g) unsalted butter, melted

½ cup (120 g) plain yogurt

¼ cup (60 ml) milk

1 tsp. (5 g) vanilla

2 cups raspberries (I use fresh, but frozen work just as well)

Some mornings call for something simple and sweet—like a warm raspberry muffin fresh out of the oven. These little gems remind me of those quiet moments before the day begins, when the lodge is still hushed. Each bite strikes the perfect balance of flavors, where the subtly sweet muffin base lets the bright, tart raspberries shine through. Topped with a buttery streusel, these muffins offer a satisfying crunch that perfectly complements their soft, tender crumb.

1. Preheat the oven to 375°F (190°C). Prepare a standard 12-cup muffin tin by greasing it with nonstick spray or lining it with paper liners. This ensures the muffins will pop out easily once baked.

2. Prepare the streusel topping first. In a bowl, mix the flour and brown sugar, then rub in the cold butter with your fingertips (or a pastry cutter) until it forms a crumbly, coarse mixture.

3. Sift the flour into a large bowl. Add the baking soda, baking powder, cinnamon, salt, and brown sugar. Stir well to combine and ensure the leavening agents are evenly distributed.

4. In a separate bowl, crack the eggs and beat them until well combined. Add the banana, melted butter, yogurt, milk, and vanilla. Stir until the mixture is smooth and creamy—this is the heart of your muffin batter.

5. Mix the dry ingredients into the wet ingredients until just combined. Avoid overmixing to keep the batter light.

6. Gently fold in the raspberries, taking care not to crush them—those little berries are like delicate snowflakes, so handle them with love.

7. Spoon the batter into the prepared muffin tin, filling each cup about two-thirds full. The muffins will rise beautifully in the oven!

8. Generously sprinkle the streusel topping over the batter. Think of it like decorating your muffins with a festive, crunchy crown.

9. Bake the muffins for 15 to 18 minutes, or until a toothpick inserted into the center comes out clean. Your kitchen will soon smell like a bakery!

10. Once baked, remove the muffins from the oven and allow them to cool in the tin for about 15 minutes. Then, transfer them to a wire rack to cool completely (if you can wait that long!)

VEGAN BANANA BREAD

SERVES

10–12

½ cup (100 g) brown sugar

¼ cup (100 g) white sugar

⅓ cup (80 ml) coconut oil, at room temperature

2 tsp. (10 ml) vanilla

4 bananas (the riper, the better)

1 + ¾ cups (220 g) all-purpose flour, sifted

1 + ½ tsp. (6 g) baking powder

½ tsp. (2 g) baking soda

1 tsp. (2.6 g) ground cinnamon

⅓ cup (80 ml) plant-based milk

½ cup (60 g) walnuts or pecans, coarsely chopped

There are always a few overripe bananas in the fruit bowl—freckled, forgotten, and perfect for this loaf. No eggs, no butter, no drama—just a ridiculously good banana bread that's moist, fluffy, and gently sweet, with no compromise on flavor. Overripe bananas bring a deep, caramelized richness that means there's no need for extra sugar in this wholesome plant-based treat. Made with pantry staples and minimal effort, it's the kind of thing you can throw together before first lifts and enjoy after the last run.

1. Preheat the oven to 350°F (175°C). Grease a 9 x 5-inch (23 x 13 cm) loaf pan with a bit of soft butter and dust it with flour. This handy trick will help your banana bread slide right out when it's done.

2. In a bowl, stir together the brown and white sugars. This blend gives a more nuanced sweetness to your banana bread.

3. Add the coconut oil and vanilla to the sugars, stirring until well combined.

4. In a separate bowl, mash those ripe bananas with a fork until they're at a chunky applesauce consistency. This is where all that natural sweetness and flavor comes in!

5. Pour the bananas into the sugar mixture, stirring until everything is fully blended.

6. In a separate bowl, whisk together the flour, baking powder, baking soda, and cinnamon.

7. Gradually add the dry ingredients to the banana mixture, stirring gently. Take it easy here; we don't want to overmix—this is the secret to keeping your bread light and airy.

8. Stir in the plant milk until just combined. This helps keep the batter moist and tender.

9. Gently fold in the walnuts or pecans for a delightful crunch in every bite.

10. Pour the batter into your prepared pan, spreading it evenly. Bake for 50 to 60 minutes or until a toothpick inserted into the center comes out clean. The top should be a lovely golden brown and hard to resist!

11. Let the banana bread cool in the pan for 10 minutes, then transfer to a wire rack to cool completely.

DOUBLE CHOCOLATE BANANA BREAD

SERVES
8–10

3 bananas (the riper, the better)
½ cup (113 g) unsalted butter, melted
¾ cup (150 g) brown sugar
1 egg
1 tsp. (5 g) vanilla
1 cup (120 g) all-purpose flour
1 tsp. (2.6 g) ground cinnamon
1 tsp. (5 g) baking soda
½ cup (50 g) cocoa powder
1 cup (170 g) chocolate chunks

There is something about bananas and chocolate that just works. This loaf has become one of my personal favorites, and honestly, I've lost count of how many times I've shared this recipe. Yes, it is indulgent, but also wholesome. Packed with potassium, vitamin C, and dietary fiber, it combines the benefits of ripe bananas with the rich, satisfying taste of chocolate. The secret to this perfect loaf is using overripe bananas, which not only enhance the sweetness but also give it an incredibly moist texture. As a lodge tradition, these always make their way into the guests' lunch boxes after breakfast—perfect for a midday treat on the slopes!

1. Preheat the oven to 350°F (175°C). Grease a 9 x 5-inch (23 x 13 cm) loaf pan and line it with parchment paper, making sure the parchment overhangs on the sides. This will act as a sling to easily lift the bread out later.

2. In a large bowl, mash the bananas with a fork until they're mushy but still have some chunky bits. This adds texture to the loaf.

3. Stir in the butter, followed by the brown sugar, egg, and vanilla. Mix until everything is fully combined and smooth.

4. In a separate bowl, sift the flour, cinnamon, baking soda, and cocoa powder. Now, gently fold this dry mixture into the banana mixture. Think of it as a delicate dance—not a wrestling match! Be gentle here; you do not want to overmix if you want a light and fluffy loaf.

5. Next, toss in those glorious chocolate chunks and give it a quick stir. Because let's be honest: Chocolate Makes everything better, right?

6. Pour the mixture into the prepared pan and bake for 35 to 40 minutes, or until a toothpick inserted in the center comes out clean. Check after 30 minutes as ovens can vary. A chocolate smear is expected, so don't be alarmed if you hit a gooey chocolate pocket. Consider it a bonus!

7. Once your kitchen is filled with the heavenly aroma of banana bread, allow it to cool in the pan for 10 minutes before turning it out onto a cooling rack.

HEALTHY ZUCCHINI BREAD WITH PRUNES AND CHOCOLATE CHIPS

SERVES
16–18

3 eggs

3 cups (300 g) zucchini, shredded and excess moisture squeezed out

½ cup (120 ml) neutral oil (avocado, light olive oil)

½ cup (120 ml) applesauce

½ cup (300 g) brown sugar

1 tbsp. (15 ml) vanilla extract

2 cups (250 g) all-purpose flour

1 cup (100 g) ground almonds

1 tsp. (2.6 g) ground cinnamon

1 tsp. (4 g) baking soda

1 tsp. (4 g) baking powder

¼ tsp. (1.5 g) salt

¾ cup (130 g) chocolate chips

½ cup (85 g) prunes, pitted and chopped

Get ready to power up for your day on the slopes with this healthier twist on classic zucchini bread. It all started to use up a few too many zucchinis left in the lodge fridge—but what came out of the oven was such a hit! Packed with wholesome ingredients, this delightful loaf is a guilt-free indulgence. Moist zucchini adds a boost of vitamins while keeping each slice wonderfully tender, and the prunes bring a natural sweetness and chewy texture that elevate the flavor. I couldn't resist throwing in some chocolate chips for that bit of indulgence.

1. Preheat the oven to 350°F (175°C). Prepare two 9 x 5-inch (23 x 13 cm) loaf pans by greasing and lining them with parchment paper—this will ensure your bread slides right out when it's done!

2. In a large bowl, crack the eggs and beat them until fully combined. Then stir in the zucchini, oil, applesauce, brown sugar, and vanilla. Mix until everything is harmoniously blended—like a perfect run down a mountain!

3. Sift the flour into another bowl. Add the almonds, cinnamon, baking soda, baking powder, and salt. Stir well to combine, ensuring all the dry ingredients are evenly distributed.

4. Gently fold the dry ingredients into the wet mixture, stirring until just combined. Be careful not to overmix to keep the bread light and moist.

5. Gradually fold in the chocolate chips and prunes. These will add both sweetness and texture to each bite.

6. Pour the batter into the prepared loaf pans and spread it evenly. Bake for 45 to 55 minutes. To check if the bread is ready, insert a toothpick into the center of a loaf. If it comes out clean, you've reached the perfect finish line!

7. Remove the loaves from the oven and let them cool in the pans for about 15 minutes. Then, carefully transfer them to a cooling rack.

MAKES
12 MUFFINS

2 cups (250 g) all-purpose flour

¾ cup (150 g) brown sugar

1 tsp. (4 g) baking powder

2 tsp. (5.2 g) ground cinnamon

¼ tsp. (1.5 g) salt

¾ cup + 1 tbsp. (200 g) unsalted butter, melted

2 eggs

1 tsp. (5 g) vanilla

3 overripe bananas, mashed

1 cup (85 g) oatmeal

1 cup (90 g) unsweetened flaked coconut

½ cup (60 g) walnuts, coarsely chopped

¾ cup (130 g) chocolate chips

1 banana, sliced (for topping)

2 tbsp. (30 g) demerara sugar (for topping)

BANANA OATMEAL MUFFINS WITH WALNUTS AND CHOCOLATE

These muffins are my go-to when the day ahead is full of action—or when I just want something cozy with my coffee. They're packed with ripe bananas (always a few hanging around the fruit bowl), hearty oats, and crunchy walnuts for that "I'm being healthy" energy. But let's be honest—it's the chocolate chips that keep me coming back. Just enough to make them feel like a treat, and a bit decadent, without tipping into dessert territory. These muffins are nourishing, not too sweet, and sturdy enough to toss in a backpack for mid-run snack breaks.

1. Preheat the oven to 350°F (175°C). Let it warm up like a cozy lodge fireplace after a day on the slopes. Next, coat a 12-cup standard muffin tin with butter or nonstick spray, or line it with paper liners.

2. In a large bowl, combine the flour, brown sugar, baking powder, cinnamon, and salt. Whisk it all together like you're stirring up a snowstorm.

3. Melt the butter and let it cool, then whisk the eggs with the vanilla and stir in the bananas until everything comes together.

4. Pour the butter and the egg banana mixture into the bowl with the dry ingredients. Stir gently until everything is combined, being careful not to overmix, as your muffins might turn out denser than a packed snowball.

5. Gently fold in the oatmeal, coconut, walnuts, and chocolate chips. These ingredients bring texture, flavor, and a touch of indulgence.

6. Divide the batter evenly among the 12 muffin cups, filling each about ¾ of the way. Top each muffin with a slice of banana and a sprinkle of demerara sugar for a crunchy, sweet finish.

7. Bake the muffins for about 18 to 20 minutes. Let the scent of warm bananas, cinnamon, and melting chocolate fill your kitchen, bringing that ski lodge ambiance right to your home. They're done when a toothpick inserted in the center comes out clean and the tops are golden brown—like a perfect après-ski tan.

8. Let the muffins cool in the tin for a few minutes, then transfer them onto a wire rack to cool completely.

EAT, SKI & REPEAT

"LONG TIME COMING" MORNING GLORY MUFFINS

MAKES
12 MUFFINS

2 cups (250 g) all-purpose flour

¾ cup (150 g) brown sugar

1 tbsp. (15 g) baking powder

1 tsp. (5 g) baking soda

2 tsp. (10 g) ground cinnamon

¼ tsp. (1.5 g) salt

1 apple, peeled, cored, and finely shredded

2 cups (220 g) shredded carrots

½ cup (80 g) raisins

½ cup (60 g) walnuts, chopped

½ cup (40 g) unsweetened flaked coconut

¾ cup (180 ml) applesauce

½ cup (120 ml) coconut oil, at room temperature

1 tbsp. (15 ml) vanilla

Kick-start your day with a burst of flavor and energy! These muffins are as iconic as the Long Time Coming run at K3—steep, sunny, and full of zest. Just like that thrilling descent, they pack a punch with wholesome ingredients like grated carrots, juicy apples, plump raisins, and crunchy walnuts. Rich in nutrients and natural sweetness, they offer the perfect balance of flavors to fuel your morning adventure.

1. Preheat the oven to 350°F (175°C). Grease a 12-cup muffin tin or line the cups with paper liners to prevent sticking.

2. In a large bowl, combine the flour, brown sugar, baking powder, baking soda, cinnamon, and salt. Stir well to evenly distribute the dry ingredients. This step creates a light and airy base for your muffins, ensuring they rise perfectly.

3. Stir in the apple, carrots, raisins, walnuts, and coconut. These ingredients not only boost flavor but also provide a nutritious, energy-packed punch, perfect for your day on the slopes.

4. In a separate bowl, whisk together the applesauce, coconut oil, and vanilla until well combined. This mixture adds moisture and a natural sweetness, keeping your muffins soft and delicious.

5. Gently pour the wet ingredients into the dry mixture and stir until just moistened. Be careful not to overmix—overmixing can lead to dense muffins. A few lumps are perfectly fine.

6. Spoon the batter into the prepared muffin cups, filling each about two-thirds full. This ensures the muffins will have enough room to rise without overflowing.

7. Bake the muffins for 18 to 20 minutes, or until the tops spring back when lightly pressed. Keep an eye on them, as baking times can vary depending on your oven.

8. Let the muffins cool in the tin for about 5 minutes before transferring them to a wire rack to cool completely. This step allows the muffins to set, making them easier to handle.

FIRST TRACKS BREAKFASTS

Days in the mountains demand a hearty start. When you're shredding powder or trekking through snow, you're burning serious calories—and starting on an empty stomach just won't cut it. Your body needs fuel, and good nutrition is key to keeping your energy up and your spirits high. These breakfast recipes aren't just designed to lure you out of bed—they're built to power your day and keep you cruising down the slopes, not crashing before lunch.

COCONUT OATMEAL

This oatmeal blends creamy comfort with tropical flair—a little taste of paradise perfect for snowy mountain mornings. Made with coconut milk, topped with toasted coconut flakes, and drizzled with maple syrup, it delivers healthy fats, fiber, and natural sweetness to keep you going strong. It's warm, hearty, and a little unexpected—just like Shannon, one of our boldest ski guides. Adventurous, creative, and always thinking outside the lines, Shannon swears by this oatmeal to power her runs. Skiing with her is never ordinary—it's always an adventure.

SERVES

4

2 cups (180 g) rolled oats
1 + ⅔ cups (400 ml) coconut cream
2 cups (480 ml) water
2 tbsp. (30 ml) maple syrup or honey
1 tsp. vanilla extract
¼ tsp. salt
¼ cup (25 g) shredded coconut

1. In a medium saucepan, combine the rolled oats, coconut cream, water, maple syrup or honey, vanilla, and salt.
2. Bring the mixture to a gentle simmer over low to medium heat, stirring occasionally to prevent sticking.
3. Let the oats cook for 8 to 10 minutes, stirring occasionally, until they've absorbed the liquid and reached a soft, creamy texture. For a thinner consistency, add a splash more water or coconut cream until you reach your desired texture.
4. While the oats cook, heat a small skillet over medium heat. Add the coconut, stirring frequently for 2 to 3 minutes, until it turns golden and fragrant. (Keep a close eye here to prevent burning.)
5. Spoon the oatmeal into four bowls, then top with the coconut. Add your favorite fruits for extra flavor: Try banana slices or mango for a tropical touch or fresh berries for a burst of brightness.

"LADIES FIRST" OVERNIGHT OATS

SERVES

4

2 cups (180 g) old-fashioned rolled oats

2 cups (480 ml) milk (dairy or nondairy)

2 tbsp. (28 g) chia seeds

2 tbsp. (15 g) chopped walnuts

¼ cup (25 g) shredded coconut

1 tbsp. (15 ml) vanilla extract

1 tbsp. (18 g) golden raisins

2 tbsp. (30 ml) honey or maple syrup (adjust to taste)

½ tsp. ground cinnamon

Pinch of sea salt

1 cup (250 g) plain Greek yogurt

This delightful dish is as effortless as hitting the snooze button yet as bold as the Ladies First run at K3. It's named after a plucky lady who was the first to drop into that line—she triggered a mini avalanche, ended up waist-deep at the bottom, and still managed to dig herself out with pure grit. Like her, this breakfast is all about determination with zero fuss: Just mix everything the night before, pop it in the fridge, and wake up to a wholesome, ready-to-go meal.

1. In a large bowl, combine the oats, milk, chia seeds, walnuts, coconut, golden raisins, vanilla, honey (or maple syrup, cinnamon, and a pinch of salt. Stir well until everything is fully incorporated.

2. Cover the bowl and refrigerate overnight (or for at least 4 hours) to allow the oats to soak up the flavors and soften to perfection.

3. In the morning, remove the mixture from the fridge and gently fold in the yogurt until the oats are creamy and luscious. This step helps keep the oats fresh while adding a rich, smooth texture. The golden raisins will have plumped up overnight, giving you a sweet surprise in every bite.

4. Spoon the oats into four jars or bowls and top with your favorite extras—whether it's more walnuts, coconut, fresh fruit, or a drizzle of nut butter, the choice is yours!

ORANGE AND YOGURT PANCAKES

SERVES

2-3

1 + ½ cup (180 g) all-purpose flour

¾ tsp. baking powder

1 + ½ tsp. baking soda

¼ tsp. salt

1 tbsp. (30 g) brown sugar

2 eggs

1 + ½ cups (360 g) plain Greek yogurt

½ cup (120 ml) milk

Zest of 1 orange, minced

½ cup (120 ml) freshly squeezed orange juice

1 tbsp. (14 g) unsalted butter, for cooking

There are always pancakes on the breakfast table at the lodge—fluffy stacks just waiting to be devoured before the day begins. These orange and yogurt pancakes are a fresh twist on a classic, with a zing of orange zest and the creamy tang of yogurt. In fact, this recipe is the favorite of a group of skiers from Utah who swear by two things: the powder at K3 and pancakes for breakfast. They claim the snow here is "otherworldly" (and trust us, they've seen their share of powder), but it's the pancakes that keep them coming back for more. Who can blame them? A plate of these beauties, and they're ready to conquer the mountain!

1. In a large bowl, whisk together the flour, baking powder, baking soda, salt, and brown sugar. This is where all the fluffiness begins.

2. In a separate bowl, beat the eggs, then add the yogurt, milk, orange zest, and orange juice. Mix until smooth and well combined. Smell that orange? It's a burst of sunshine!

3. Pour the wet ingredients into the dry mixture and stir gently until just combined—don't worry about a few lumps; they're key to keeping the pancakes light and fluffy.

4. Heat a nonstick skillet or griddle over medium heat and melt a little butter.

5. Spoon about ¼ cup (60 ml) batter onto the skillet. Cook until bubbles form on the surface, then flip and cook until golden brown on the other side. Repeat with the remaining batter.

6. Stack up those fluffy beauties and finish with a generous drizzle of maple syrup, fresh berries, or a sprinkle of powdered sugar for a touch of citrusy sweetness.

LEMON RICOTTA PANCAKES

SERVES
4

1 + ¾ cups (220 g) all-purpose flour

¼ cup (50 g) sugar

2 tsp. baking powder

1 tsp. baking soda

¼ tsp. salt

Juice of 2 lemons

Zest of 1 lemon, finely minced

1 + ½ cups (360 ml) whole milk

1 + ½ cups (375 g) ricotta cheese

2 eggs

1 tsp. vanilla

2 tbsp. (30 ml) melted unsalted butter, for cooking

These zesty pancakes are a bright, citrusy take on a refined favorite. With the fresh lift of lemon zest and the creamy richness of ricotta, each bite is as invigorating as a crisp mountain morning. I love using ricotta—it brings a soft, milky decadence that Makes these pancakes feel extra special. This recipe is dedicated to Todd, our lead mountain guide. He's the kind of person who nudges you just beyond your comfort zone, yet always Makes you feel like a hero. His ski lines are bold, creative, and a little unexpected—just like these pancakes.

1. In a large bowl, whisk together the flour, sugar, baking powder, baking soda, and salt until well combined. Set aside.

2. In a separate bowl, combine the lemon juice, lemon zest, milk, ricotta, eggs, and vanilla. Whisk until the mixture is thick and creamy.

3. Gently fold the wet ingredients into the dry ingredients, stirring just until combined—don't worry if the batter is a bit lumpy! Avoid overmixing to keep the pancakes light and fluffy.

4. Heat a griddle or large skillet over medium heat and lightly coat with melted butter.

5. Pour ¼ cup batter for each pancake onto the griddle, spacing them apart to prevent spreading. Cook for about 3 minutes, or until bubbles form on the surface and begin to pop. Flip and cook the other side until golden brown, about 1 to 2 minutes more.

SERVES

2–3

1 + ¼ cups (150 g) all-purpose flour

1 tsp. (4 g) baking powder

½ tsp. (2.5 g) baking soda

½ tsp. (2.5 g) salt

1 egg

1 + ½ cups (360 ml) buttermilk

3 tbsp. (45 ml) honey

1 tbsp. (14 g) unsalted butter, for cooking

OLD-FASHIONED BUTTERMILK PANCAKES

These golden delights strike the perfect balance between light and hearty—and they never go out of style. With their tangy buttermilk flavor and melt-in-your-mouth texture, they're just like Grandma used to make—if Grandma ran a ski lodge. They're also a firm favorite of our housekeepers, Thea and Isabelle, who swear these pancakes give them the energy they need to power through changeover days.

1. In a large bowl, whisk together the flour, baking powder, baking soda, and salt until well combined.

2. In a separate bowl, lightly beat the egg, then add the buttermilk and honey, whisking until smooth and creamy.

3. Gently pour the wet ingredients into the dry ingredients, stirring just until combined—don't worry about a few lumps; they'll make for extra-fluffy pancakes!

4. Heat a nonstick skillet or griddle over medium heat and lightly grease with a bit of butter or oil. Pour ¼ cup (60 ml) batter per pancake onto the griddle.

5. Cook until bubbles form on the surface and the edges look set, then flip and cook the other side until golden brown. Repeat with the remaining batter.

"EUPHORIA" COCONUT CREPES

SERVES
4–6

1 cup (120 g) all-purpose flour

¼ cup (50 g) granulated sugar

2 tsp. (9 g) coconut oil

1 + ⅔ cups (400 ml) full fat coconut milk (from a can)

2 eggs

1 tsp. (5 g) vanilla

¼ cup (60 ml) milk

Zest of 1 lime

1 tbsp. (14 g) butter (for cooking)

½ cup (25 g) flaked coconut (for garnish)

Who says you can't chase powder and paradise at the same time? These coconut crepes bring a splash of island sunshine to the snowy peaks—because even the chilliest mornings deserve a little tropical indulgence. Inspired by the smooth, sweeping curves of the Euphoria run at K3, these crepes mirror its graceful lines—folded, rolled, or artfully draped on the plate, they echo the elegant flow of that unforgettable descent. Whether you're fueling up for a day on the slopes or simply savoring the moment, they deliver a taste of faraway shores—no passport required.

1. Before you get started, make sure all your ingredients are at room temperature. Trust me, it'll make everything mix so much better.

2. In a bowl, whisk the flour and sugar until combined. Add the coconut oil and stir until everything's smooth and well-blended—no lumps allowed!

3. Slowly pour in the coconut milk, followed by the eggs, vanilla, and milk. Whisk it all until the batter is silky smooth.

4. If you're chasing crepe perfection, pass the batter through a sieve to catch any sneaky lumps. It's optional, but if you love ultra-smooth, melt-in-your-mouth crepes, it's worth the extra step.

5. Grab a nonstick pan or crepe pan and set it over medium heat. Take a piece of kitchen towel, dip it in butter, and swipe it across the pan for a light, even coating. Once the pan is hot (but not smoking), you're in business!

6. Pour ¼ cup (60 ml) batter into the pan, then quickly tilt and swirl to spread it into a thin, even circle. Let it cook for 1 to 2 minutes, until the edges lift slightly and the bottom turns golden.

7. Pro tip: The first crepe is always a bit of a test run—think of it as your practice round! Use it to test the batter. If it's too thick, stir in a splash more milk to loosen it up. No stress—the best ones are yet to come!

8. Gently loosen the edges with a spatula, then flip with confidence! Cook for another 30 seconds on the other side until lightly golden. Slide it onto a plate and repeat with the rest of the batter.

9. Once your crepes are ready, finely grate the lime zest on top for a refreshing citrusy kick—add it at the end to keep the flavor bright and zesty, sprinkle with flaked coconut, and you are ready to roll (or fold and devour).

MEXICAN-INSPIRED SCRAMBLED EGGS

SERVES

4

1 red bell pepper

8 eggs

1 small onion, finely chopped

2 Roma tomatoes, diced

1 cup (113 g) shredded sharp cheddar cheese

1 tbsp. (14 g) unsalted butter

Fresh cilantro, chopped (for garnish)

Sea salt and freshly ground black pepper to taste

Hot sauce (optional, for extra kick)

These fluffy eggs mingle with juicy tomatoes, sautéed onions, smoky roasted red peppers, and sharp, melty cheddar cheese to take your morning to the next level. I'm often asked how the eggs turn out so fluffy—well, that's a lodge secret I'm happy to share: It's all in the gentle folding and just the right amount of heat. Low and slow is the name of the game. The richness of the roasted red peppers and creamy cheddar cheese pairs perfectly with the freshness of the tomatoes and a final sprinkle of cilantro.

1. First, roast the red pepper. This step adds a smoky, slightly sweet depth that takes the dish to the next level. You can char the pepper under the broiler until the skin blisters or roast it in the oven at 450°F (230°C) for about 15 to 20 minutes.

2. Once the pepper is beautifully charred, place it in a bowl and cover with plastic wrap or a plate to let it steam for about 10 minutes. This makes peeling off the skin a breeze. Once it's cool enough to handle, remove the skin, discard the seeds, chop it up, and set aside.

3. Next, heat the butter in a large pan over medium heat. Add the onion and sauté until soft and translucent, about 5 minutes. Toss in the tomatoes and roasted red pepper, stirring for another 2 to 3 minutes until the tomatoes begin to soften and release their juices.

4. Crack the eggs into a bowl, season with a pinch of salt and pepper, and whisk until smooth and slightly frothy.

5. Pour the eggs into the pan with the vegetables and gently stir, keeping the heat on medium to prevent overcooking. As the eggs begin to set, continue stirring gently to create soft, creamy curds. When they're almost done but still slightly runny, sprinkle in the cheddar cheese. Stir just until the cheese melts into the eggs, giving them a velvety texture. Take care not to overcook—remove from the heat while the eggs are still soft and creamy to keep them tender, not rubbery.

6. Serve the scrambled eggs on a plate, garnished with extra cilantro for a fresh, herby finish. For an extra kick, drizzle with hot sauce or serve alongside salsa for added flavor.

"INTO THE MYSTIC" EGGS BENEDICT

SERVES
4

HOLLANDAISE SAUCE

¼ cup (60 ml) white wine

¼ cup (60 ml) white wine vinegar

1 tbsp. (10 g) finely chopped shallots

1 fresh thyme sprig

1 tsp. (2 g) black peppercorns

3 large egg yolks

½ cup (113 g) unsalted butter, melted and warm

1 tbsp. (15 ml) freshly squeezed lemon juice

Sea salt and freshly ground black pepper (to taste)

Pinch of cayenne pepper (optional)

EGGS BENEDICT

4 slices Canadian bacon (or your choice of ham)

2 English muffins (split in half)

4 eggs

Splash of white vinegar (for poaching the eggs)

Fresh chives or parsley (for garnish)

Paprika (for garnish)

Sea salt and freshly ground black pepper to taste

This classic breakfast is like the culinary version of cruising down a black diamond run—bold, exciting, and oh so satisfying. But if there's one ski run that truly captures the spirit of eggs Benedict, it's Into the Mystic at K3—wide open, steep, and so breathtaking it feels like a fresh start. A toasted English muffin as your sturdy base, a layer of salty Canadian bacon bringing just the right amount of edge, and a perfectly poached egg. And the hollandaise? It's as smooth and velvety as that first effortless glide down untouched snow.

Not only is this dish an indulgent way to start your day, but it's also surprisingly balanced. The eggs deliver a hit of protein to keep your legs steady; the Canadian bacon is a lighter yet savory touch, and the luxurious hollandaise? That's your well-earned reward.

1. In a small saucepan, simmer wine, vinegar, shallots, thyme and peppercorns until reduced to 2 tablespoons (5 to 7 minutes). Strain and set aside.

2. In a heatproof bowl, whisk together the egg yolks and the vinegar reduction until well combined.

3. Set bowl over simmering water; whisk 3 to 5 minutes until thick. Gradually whisk in butter until creamy then add lemon juice and season to taste.

4. Toast the English muffins until golden brown. Then cook the Canadian bacon in a skillet over medium heat until it's heated through and slightly crispy on the edges, about 2 to 3 minutes per side.

5. Fill a medium pot with 3 inches of water; bring to a boil, then reduce to a gentle simmer (small bubbles, not rolling). Add a splash of vinegar to help the whites hold together.

6. Crack one egg into a small bowl, then gently slide it into the simmering water. Repeat with the remaining eggs. Poach the eggs for about 3 to 4 minutes, or until the whites are set but the yolks remain runny. Remove with a slotted spoon and drain on paper towels.

7. Top each English muffin half with a layer of Canadian bacon, followed by a poached egg. Generously drizzle with warm hollandaise sauce and season with salt and pepper. Garnish with chives or parsley for that extra flair.

"BROTHERLY LOVE" HUEVOS RANCHEROS

SERVES
4

Wake up to a fiesta on your plate with huevos rancheros—the ultimate morning adventure for taste buds ready to hit the slopes! Just like the Brotherly Love run at K3, this dish is steep, deep, and guaranteed to get your adrenaline pumping. Imagine sunny-side-up eggs perched on crispy flour tortillas, smothered in a zesty ranchero sauce as bold as that first drop-in. But the real kicker? Smoky, spiced chorizo beans that bring a rich, savory depth to every bite. The textures are a thrill ride—crunchy tortillas, velvety yolks, and those hearty beans, all finished with fresh cilantro, creamy avocado, and a sprinkle of crumbled feta cheese. It's the perfect fuel for tackling big lines and chasing powder—one bite, and you're diving in, no hesitation.

RANCHERO SAUCE

1 tbsp. (15 ml) olive oil

1 medium onion, finely chopped

2 garlic cloves, minced

1 jalapeño, diced (optional, adjust to spice preference)

1 tsp. (2 g) ground cumin

1 tsp. (2 g) smoked paprika

½ tsp. (1 g) chili powder

½ cup (400 g) diced tomatoes

Sea salt and freshly ground black pepper to taste

CHORIZO AND BLACK BEANS

½ tbsp. (7.5 ml) olive oil

1 chorizo sausage (Mexican style), casing removed and crumbled

½ medium onion, finely diced

2 garlic cloves, minced

½ tsp. (1 g) ground cumin

¼ tsp. (.5 g) smoked paprika

Sea salt and freshly ground black pepper to taste

1 cup cooked black beans (or ½ can, drained and rinsed)

2 tbsp. (30 ml) chicken or vegetable broth (optional, for a saucier consistency)

8 small flour tortillas

8 large eggs

TOPPINGS

Avocado slices

Crumbled feta

Fresh cilantro, chopped

Lime wedges (optional)

Sliced jalapeños (optional, for extra heat)

RANCHERO SAUCE

1. Heat the olive oil in a medium skillet over medium heat. Add the onion and garlic, cooking gently until soft and fragrant, about 5 to 7 minutes.

2. Add the jalapeño (if using) for a bit of heat. Sprinkle in the cumin, smoked paprika, and chili powder, stirring well. Cook for 1 to 2 minutes, until the spices bloom and become aromatic.

3. Stir in the tomatoes, bring the sauce to a simmer, and cook for 10 minutes, stirring occasionally, until it thickens slightly. Season with salt and pepper to taste. Remove from the heat and set aside.

CHORIZO AND BLACK BEANS

4. Heat the olive oil in a large skillet over medium heat. Crumble the chorizo into the pan and cook, stirring occasionally, until browned and slightly crispy, about 5 to 7 minutes.

5. Add the onion to the skillet with the chorizo and cook for 3 to 4 minutes, until softened. Add the garlic and cook for another 1 to 2 minutes, stirring frequently.

6. Stir in the cumin, smoked paprika, and a pinch of salt and pepper. Add the black beans, stirring to combine. For a saucier consistency, add 2 tablespoons of chicken or vegetable broth. Let the mixture simmer for 3 to 5 minutes, allowing the flavors to meld. Taste and adjust the seasoning, adding more salt, pepper, or cumin if needed.

TORTILLAS

7   In a large skillet, heat a thin layer of olive oil over medium-high heat. Fry each tortilla for 1 to 2 minutes per side, until golden and slightly crispy on the edges but still soft in the center. Place the fried tortillas on a plate lined with paper towels to drain excess oil.

EGGS

8   In the same skillet, cook the eggs sunny side up (or to your preference), ensuring the yolks remain runny for that luscious, oozy finish.

ASSEMBLE

9   Place two tortillas on each plate. Spoon the black bean and chorizo mixture over the tortillas, spreading it out evenly. Top each with a fried egg.

10 Spoon the ranchero sauce generously over the eggs. Add the avocado slices, sprinkle with the feta cheese, and garnish with cilantro. Serve with lime wedges and extra jalapeños for a final kick, if desired.

APRÈS-SKI FIRESIDE APPETIZERS

A day of cat skiing isn't complete without a warm, welcoming spread waiting back at the lodge. After carving through powder all day, you'll be ready to replace those hard-earned burned calories with something delicious—ideally by the fire, with a drink in hand. Whether it's something bubbly or a mug of something steamy, après-ski is all about swapping stories and refueling in style. This chapter brings together the most-requested lodge favorites—comforting, crowd-pleasing bites perfect for sharing after a day on the slopes.

PERFECTLY SMOOTH HUMMUS

SERVES

4

HUMMUS

1 ½ cups (360 g) canned chickpeas, drained and rinsed

½ tsp. (2.5 g) baking soda

½ cup (120 g) tahini

¼ cup (60 ml) freshly squeezed lemon juice

1 garlic clove, minced

½ tsp. (1 g) ground cumin

Sea salt (to taste)

2 tbsp. (30 ml) olive oil (plus more for drizzling)

4 tbsp. water as needed for consistency

TOPPINGS

Olive oil

Paprika, cumin, and/or parsley

Toasted pine nuts

Skiing is all about smooth turns, effortless glides, and the perfect finish—just like this hummus. This isn't your average store-bought spread; it's a velvety, rich, and ridiculously creamy dip that deserves a place next to the crackling fire. The secret? A perfect balance of tahini and lemon, and just enough olive oil to make it silky smooth. Speaking of smooth, Natascha, one of our cat drivers, handles the mountain like a pro—her driving is so seamless and steady, it's as flawless as this hummus. Together, they make every ride and every bite a total pleasure.

1. For ultra-smooth hummus, start by softening the chickpeas. Place them in a saucepan with the baking soda, cover with water, and bring to a boil. Let them simmer for 10 to 15 minutes until they become extra tender and some skins start to loosen. This step helps create that irresistibly creamy texture. Once done, drain the chickpeas and rinse them under cold water, removing any loose skins for an even silkier finish.

2. While the chickpeas cool, start with the foundation of great hummus: tahini and lemon juice. In a food processor, blend the tahini with the lemon juice for about 30 seconds until it turns pale, light, and airy—like fresh mountain powder.

3. Now, bring in the bold, cozy flavors. Add the garlic, cumin, and salt. Give it another spin to evenly distribute those warm, toasty notes.

4. Time to bring it all together! Add the warm chickpeas to the tahini mixture and start blending. Drizzle in the olive oil as the mixture comes together. Slowly add the cold water, one spoonful at a time, until the hummus is as smooth as a freshly groomed ski run. Keep the food processor running for 2 to 3 minutes—the longer, the silkier.

5. Take a taste (no double-dipping—unless it's just for you!). Need more zing? Add a squeeze of lemon. A little extra depth? Another pinch of salt. Blend once more to lock in the perfect balance.

6. Scoop your velvety hummus into a bowl and create a swirl with the back of a spoon. Drizzle with the olive oil; sprinkle with paprika, cumin, or parsley; and for a little crunch, add the pine nuts. Now, all that's left is to grab warm pita or crisp veggies and dig in—because après-ski snacks should always be this smooth.

APRÈS-SKI FLAT BREADS

SERVES
4

½ cup (120 ml) extra-virgin olive oil

2 garlic cloves, minced

1 cup (120 g) shredded mozzarella cheese

4 small flatbreads or naan (store-bought or homemade)

½ cup (75 g) crumbled feta

½ cup (80 g) sun-dried tomatoes, sliced

4 slices prosciutto

½ cup (small handful) arugula

¼ cup (60 ml) balsamic glaze

Sea salt and freshly ground black pepper to taste

Red pepper flakes (optional)

These warm, crispy flatbreads are especially great when guests come back early, and I'm caught off guard. No problem! I can throw these into the oven in a flash, and within minutes, they're golden and ready to serve. Whether I'm rushing to feed a hungry skier or looking for a quick, comforting snack, these flatbreads never disappoint. I can top them with everything from rich cheeses and savory prosciutto to fresh veggies and tangy sauces, and they're always a hit. They're the ultimate last-minute lifesaver!

1. Preheat the oven to 400°F (200°C).

2. In a small bowl, mix the olive oil, garlic, salt, and pepper. Brush this garlicky goodness over each flatbread.

3. Next, sprinkle a layer of mozzarella over the flatbreads, then add the feta. Cheese lovers, feel free to be generous! Top with the sun-dried tomatoes and a slice of prosciutto—the tomatoes bring a sweet-tart flavor burst, while the prosciutto adds a savory kick.

4. Place the flatbreads directly on a baking sheet or pizza stone and bake for 8 to 10 minutes, until the cheese is melted and bubbly and the edges are golden and crisp.

5. Remove from the oven and top immediately with the arugula. The warmth of the flatbreads will gently wilt the arugula, adding a peppery freshness. Drizzle with balsamic glaze and add a sprinkle of red pepper flakes if you're feeling spicy.

SKI LODGE POTATO SKINS

SERVES
8

4 large russet potatoes, scrubbed clean

¼ cup (57 g) unsalted butter, melted

2 tbsp. (30 ml) olive oil

Sea salt and freshly ground black pepper to taste

1 cup (113 g) shredded cheddar cheese

4 slices bacon, cooked and crumbled

½ cup (120 g) sour cream

2 green onions, thinly sliced

Red pepper flakes or smoked paprika for a little kick (optional)

After a day of shredding powder, nothing says comfort like a plate of crispy potato skins, piled high and straight from the oven. Maybe it's my Polish roots speaking—but give me a potato in any form, and I'm happy. There's something about winter that Makes me crave that golden, cheesy crunch even more, especially after a full day on the mountain. These little beauties are the perfect mix of crispy edges, gooey melted cheese, smoky bacon, and a cool dollop of sour cream.

1. Preheat the oven to 400°F (200°C).

2. Pierce each potato a few times with a fork to allow steam to escape during baking. Place the potatoes on a baking tray (rather than directly on the oven rack) to catch any juices and keep your oven clean. Bake for 45 to (50 minutes, or until a knife slides easily into the center of each potato. Remove from the oven and let them cool until they're comfortable to handle.

3. Once the potatoes are cool enough, slice each one in half lengthwise. Scoop out most of the flesh, leaving about a 1/4-inch layer of potato inside each skin for structure and extra flavor. Set the potato flesh aside.

4. To get those skins perfectly crispy, arrange the potato halves back on the baking tray. Brush the insides with butter, then flip them over and brush the outsides with olive oil. Season with a bit of salt and pepper. Bake for 10 minutes to crisp up the skins.

5. Arrange the potato halves back on the baking tray, skin-side down. Fill each skin with the cheddar cheese and bacon. Return to the oven for 5 to 7 minutes, until the cheese is fully melted and bubbling.

6. Remove the hot, melty potato skins from the oven. Top each one with a dollop of sour cream and a sprinkle of green onions. For an extra flavor boost, add a pinch of red pepper flakes or a dash of smoked paprika.

LOADED CHILLI CHEESE NACHOS WITH GUACAMOLE

SERVES

4–6

CHILI

Olive oil, for cooking

1 medium onion, diced

1 red bell pepper, diced

2 garlic cloves, minced

8 oz. (225 g) ground beef (or turkey for a lighter version)

1 tbsp. (8 g) chili powder (adjust to your spice preference)

1 tsp. (2 g) ground cumin

1 tsp. (2 g) smoked paprika

1 tsp. (1 g) dried oregano

Sea salt and freshly ground black pepper to taste

1 + ½ cups (400 g) diced tomatoes, canned or fresh

¼ cup (30 g) finely chopped sun-dried tomatoes

1 + ½ cups (240 g) canned black beans, drained and rinsed

Fresh cilantro, chopped to garnish

GUACAMOLE

2 ripe avocados

1 small tomato, finely diced

½ red onion, finely diced

Juice of 1 lime

Fresh cilantro, chopped

1 tbsp. (15 g) sour cream

Sea salt and freshly ground black pepper to taste

Nothing says après-ski like a bubbling tray of chili cheese nachos—and I swear, the second they come out of the oven, the whole lodge knows. More than once, I've heard guests walk into the boot room, take one breath, and say, "It smells like nachos in here—wow!" That's when I know I've nailed it. These nachos are my go-to when I want something quick, cozy, and guaranteed to please: crispy tortilla chips layered with spicy homemade chili, melty cheese, and a big scoop of zesty guacamole. It's comfort food with serious crunch.

CHILI

1. Heat the olive oil in a medium pan over medium heat. Add the onion, red bell pepper, and garlic. Sauté until softened and fragrant, about 5 to 7 minutes.

2. Add the ground beef, breaking it apart with a wooden spoon. Cook until browned and no pink remains.

3. Stir in the chili powder, cumin, smoked paprika, oregano, salt, and pepper. Let the spices bloom for 2 minutes, stirring constantly.

4. Add the tomatoes, sun-dried tomatoes, and black beans. Stir well, then reduce the heat and let the chili simmer for 15 to 20 minutes, stirring occasionally. It should thicken beautifully.

5. Stir in the cilantro at the end for a fresh burst of flavor. Adjust seasoning to taste. Set aside.

GUACAMOLE

6. In a medium bowl, mash the avocados with a fork, leaving some chunks for texture.

7. Stir in the tomato, red onion, lime juice, cilantro, and sour cream. Season with salt and pepper to taste. Cover and set aside.

NACHOS

8. Preheat the oven to 350°F (175°C).

9. Spread half the tortilla chips in a large ovenproof dish or baking sheet. Spoon over half the chili, then sprinkle with a mix of cheddar and mozzarella cheeses.

APRÈS-SKI FIRESIDE APPETIZERS

NACHOS

1 bag (300 g) tortilla chips

½ cup (200 g) grated cheddar cheese

1 cup (100 g) grated mozzarella cheese

1–2 jalapeños, sliced (optional for extra heat)

1 small onion, finely chopped

1 medium tomato, finely chopped

Chopped fresh cilantro (for garnish)

10 Add the remaining chips, chili, and cheese. For a spicy kick, scatter jalapeños on top.

11 Bake in the oven for 10 to 12 minutes, or until the cheese is melted, bubbling, and golden.

12 Remove the nachos from the oven. Sprinkle with the tomato, onion, and cilantro.

13 Pair with the guacamole on the side or dollop it generously on top. Serve straight from the oven for that irresistible cheese pull. These nachos disappear fast, so dig in while they're hot!

51

CHICKEN QUESADILLAS WITH SALSA

CHICKEN QUESADILLAS WITH SALSA

SERVES

4

FRESH SALSA

4 ripe tomatoes, finely diced

½ red onion, finely chopped

1 jalapeño, seeds removed and finely chopped (adjust for heat)

1 small bunch of fresh cilantro, chopped (about ¼ cup)

Juice of 1 lime

1 garlic clove, minced

Sea salt to taste

1 tsp. (5 g) olive oil

CHICKEN QUESADILLAS

1 tsp. (2 g) ground cumin

1 tsp. (2 g) smoked paprika

½ tsp. (1 g) garlic powder

Sea salt and freshly ground black pepper to taste

2 boneless, skinless chicken breasts

2 tbsp. (30 ml) olive oil

1 small red onion, thinly sliced

1 bell pepper (red or green), thinly sliced

4 medium flour tortillas

2 cups (226 g) shredded cheddar or Monterey Jack cheese (or a mix)

Fresh cilantro, chopped

Sour cream, and salsa, for serving

After a day of shredding the mountain, this crispy, gooey snack is the perfect way to treat yourself. Packed with protein, carbs, and that irresistible melted cheese, it's the perfect bite to fuel you for tomorrow's adventure. Best of all, quesadillas are endlessly customizable—whether you're a carnivore, veggie lover, or spicy food enthusiast, there's a quesadilla just waiting for you to take a bite!

1. Make the salsa first, so all the fresh flavors have time to blend. In a medium bowl, combine the tomatoes, red onion, jalapeño, cilantro, and garlic. Squeeze the juice of a fresh lime over the mix, then sprinkle with a pinch of salt. For an extra silky texture, drizzle in some olive oil (optional but highly recommended!). Toss everything together, taste, and adjust the seasoning as needed. Want it spicier? Add more jalapeño. Craving more zest? Go for another squeeze of lime!

2. In a small bowl, mix the cumin, smoked paprika, garlic powder, salt, and pepper. Coat the chicken breasts evenly with the spice mix, giving them a good rub to lock in the flavor. Heat a drizzle of olive oil in a skillet over medium heat and cook the chicken for 5 to 6 minutes on each side until golden and juicy. Let it rest for a few minutes before slicing or shredding it into bite-size pieces—perfect for stuffing into your quesadilla!

3. In the same skillet (less mess, more flavor!), toss in the red onion and bell pepper. Let them sizzle away for 5 to 6 minutes until soft and caramelized. The sweetness of the veggies will add an irresistible depth of flavor to your quesadilla filling.

4. Now, it's time to assemble the magic. Lay out four tortillas, and on one half of each tortilla, sprinkle a generous amount of cheese. Layer on the seasoned chicken and sautéed veggies, then add a little more cheese (because who can resist?). Fold the empty half of the tortilla over the filling, creating a half-moon shape, ready for some skillet action.

5   Heat up a large skillet or griddle over medium heat, and carefully place one quesadilla in. Cook for 2 to 3 minutes per side until the tortilla is golden and crispy, and the cheese is a glorious gooey mess inside. Flip with confidence—this is where the magic happens! Repeat with the rest of the quesadillas.

6   Once all are cooked, slice them into wedges and sprinkle with cilantro. Serve hot with your homemade salsa and sour cream on the side.

SAUSAGE ROLLS WITH A HONEY MUSTARD DIP

SERVES

8

SAUSAGE ROLLS

1 lb. (450 g) ground pork sausage (or your favorite sausage mix)

1 small onion, finely diced

1 garlic clove, minced

1 tbsp. (3 g) chopped fresh parsley

1 tsp. (1 g) dried thyme

1 tsp. (5 g) Dijon mustard (optional, for extra flavor in the filling)

Sea salt and freshly ground black pepper to taste

Sheets of puff pastry (store-bought, thawed)

2 eggs, beaten (for egg wash)

1 tbsp. (9 g) sesame seeds or poppy seeds (optional, for topping)

HONEY MUSTARD DIP

¼ cup (60 g) Dijon mustard

1 tbsp. (15 ml) honey

1 tbsp. (15 g) mayonnaise

There's something wonderfully nostalgic about sausage rolls—they were always the first thing to disappear at parties or holiday gatherings. This grown-up version of pigs in a blanket hit all the right notes. Flaky, golden pastry wrapped around juicy, savory sausage: It's the perfect snack to warm you up from the inside out. And just when you think it can't get any better, there's that sweet and tangy honey mustard dip that takes things to the next level. Whether I'm warming up after a snowy adventure or sharing snacks with friends by the fire, these classic sausage rolls never fail to bring smiles—and maybe a little reminiscence too.

1. Preheat the oven to 400°F (200°C) and line a baking sheet with parchment paper to prepare for the deliciousness ahead.

SAUSAGE ROLLS

2. Combine the pork sausage, onion, garlic, parsley, thyme, and Dijon mustard (if using) in a bowl. Season generously with salt and pepper, then mix everything until it's beautifully blended.

3. Lay out the puff pastry sheet on a lightly floured surface, then slice in half lengthwise to create two long strips. Shape the sausage mixture into logs and place them along the center of each pastry strip.

4. Brush the pastry edges with beaten egg, fold over the sausage to make a snug parcel, and seal well. Place seam-side down on the baking tray, cut into 2-inch (5 cm) pieces, then brush with egg wash and sprinkle with sesame or poppy seeds for a golden, tasty finish.

5. Give the tops a brush with more egg wash to ensure a beautifully golden finish and sprinkle with sesame or poppy seeds for a bit of extra flair. Bake for 20 to 25 minutes, or until they're puffed up, crisped to perfection, and gorgeously golden brown.

6. While your sausage rolls are baking, whip up the honey mustard dip by whisking together Dijon mustard, honey, and mayo (if using) Taste and adjust the seasoning.

7. Once the sausage rolls have cooled slightly (good luck waiting!), dive in! Dip them into the honey mustard sauce and watch them disappear before your eyes.

SPINACH POWERED SPANAKOPITA

A flaky symphony of spinach and feta wrapped in the world's crispiest, most buttery pastry, spanakopita is proof that greens can be anything but boring. I fell in love with this Greek classic on a trip to Greece, where every bakery window seemed to glow with golden layers of phyllo. One bite and I was hooked. It is comfort food with a Mediterranean soul. Crispy on the outside, warm and savory on the inside.

MAKES

1 9-INCH (23CM) PIE

FILLING

2 tbsp. (30 ml) olive oil

2 medium onions, finely chopped

3-4 green onions, chopped

2 garlic cloves, minced

1 lb. (450 g) fresh spinach, washed and chopped

3 eggs, lightly beaten

1 cup (240 ml) heavy cream

¼ cup (25 g) grated Parmesan cheese

1 + ½ cups (280 g) crumbled feta cheese

¼ cup (8 g) chopped fresh dill (or 1 tsp. dried dill)

2 tbsp. (6 g) chopped fresh parsley

2 tsp. (10 g) freshly squeezed lemon juice

Pinch of flaked sea salt

Grind of black pepper

PHYLLO

1 package (8 oz.) phyllo dough, thawed (you'll use about 5 to 6 sheets)

⅓ cup (76 g) unsalted butter, melted (or more as needed)

1. Heat the olive oil in a large skillet over medium heat. Add both regular and green onions, letting them sizzle and soften for about 5 minutes.

2. Add the garlic and cook for another minute until fragrant.

3. Add the spinach to the skillet and cook until wilted. Once it's cooked down, drain off any excess liquid and set aside to cool.

4. In a small bowl, beat the eggs with the cream until smooth. Add the feta cheese, and parmesan then the dill, parsley, and lemon juice. Now pour the egg and cream mixture into the skillet with the spinach and stir to combine. Add the salt and pepper to taste, then set aside.

5. Preheat the oven to 350°F (175°C). Lightly grease a 9-inch (23 cm) pie dish with the melted butter.

6. Lay a sheet of phyllo in the dish and give it a good brush of melted butter. Keep layering 5 to 6 sheets of phyllo, brushing butter between each layer and letting the edges hang over the sides of the dish.

7. Spread the spinach-feta filling evenly over the phyllo layers, ensuring it's snug and evenly distributed. Fold the overhanging phyllo edges over the filling. Brush the top edges with a bit more butter. This is all about rustic charm.

8. Bake for 40 to 45 minutes, or until the phyllo is golden and crispy.

9. Let your spanakopita cool for about 10 minutes, then slice it up and serve.

"SKINNY RIDGE" QUICHE LORRAINE

EAT, SKI & REPEAT

MAKES
1 9-INCH (23CM) QUICHE

PASTRY

1 + ¼ cups (156 g) all-purpose flour

¼ tsp. (1.2 g) salt

½ cup (113 g) unsalted butter, cold and cubed

2–3 tbsp. cold water

FILLING

6–7 slices of bacon, chopped

1 large onion, finely chopped

3 eggs

¼ cup (300 ml) heavy cream (or half-and-half)

Pinch of nutmeg (optional)

Pinch of sea salt and pepper

1 cup (100 g) grated Gruyère cheese (or Swiss cheese)

When it comes to comfort with a touch of elegance, nothing beats a slice of quiche Lorraine to chase the chill away. Much like the narrow, steep thrills of the Skinny Ridge run at K3 with its daring edge, this French classic delivers a bold satisfying bite. Crispy bacon, creamy eggs, and nutty Gruyère cheese are baked to perfection in a rugged, flaky pastry crust. It's a dish that feels wildly luxurious yet familiar, offering the right balance of challenging richness and heartiness to refuel after an adventure in the snow.

1. In a large bowl, combine the flour and salt. Add the cold butter cubes and use your fingertips to rub the butter into the flour until the mixture resembles chunky breadcrumbs. Gradually add the cold water, 1 tablespoon at a time, mixing until the dough just comes together. Be gentle, overworking the dough will make it tough. For an easier method, you can pulse everything in a food processor until just combined. Shape the dough into a disk, wrap it in plastic, and chill in the fridge for about an hour.

2. Preheat the oven to 375°F (190°C). On a lightly floured surface, roll out the dough into a 10-inch (25 cm) circle. Carefully transfer it into a 9-inch (23 cm) tart pan, pressing it into the edges. Trim any excess pastry, then prick the base with a fork to prevent puffing. Chill the crust for another 15 minutes to keep it firm.

3. Line the pastry with parchment paper and fill it with pie weights (or dried beans if you're improvising). Bake the crust for 10 to 12 minutes, remove the weights, and bake for another 5 minutes until it's lightly golden. Now you've got a sturdy, crispy base ready for your quiche!

4. While the crust bakes, cook the bacon in a skillet over medium heat until crispy. Remove it from the pan and place it on a paper towel to drain—resist the urge to snack on it all before it makes it into the quiche! In the same skillet, sauté the onion in the rendered bacon fat until soft and caramelized, about 5 to 7 minutes. Drain off any excess grease.

5. To make the filling, whisk together the eggs, cream, nutmeg, and a generous pinch of salt and pepper in a large bowl. You're aiming for a silky-smooth mixture.

APRÈS-SKI FIRESIDE APPETIZERS

6 Evenly layer the crispy bacon and golden, caramelized onions over the baked crust. Next, sprinkle the Gruyère cheese generously, making sure each bite will be perfectly cheesy. Carefully pour the egg mixture over the filling, letting it slowly seep into every nook and cranny.

7 Bake for 35 to 40 minutes, until the filling is set with just a slight jiggle in the center. The top should be lightly golden and irresistibly puffy.

8 Let it cool for a few minutes for the best texture before slicing into this savory, cheesy goodness!

SERVES

6

2 ripe avocados

Juice of 1 lemon

1 tbsp. (12 ml) Tabasco sauce

Pinch of sea salt and pepper

½ cup (120 g) sour cream

½ cup (120 g) mayonnaise

1 tsp. (2 g) chili powder

1 tsp. (2 g) cumin

1 tsp. (2 g) garlic powder

1 tsp. (2 g) paprika

1 tsp. (5 g) sea salt

1 tsp. (2 g) cracked black pepper

1 can (400-450 g) refried beans

¾ cup (175 g) grated sharp cheddar cheese

¾ cup (175 g) grated mozzarella cheese

1 bunch green onions, chopped

¼ cup (60 g) chopped cilantro

½ cup (120 g) chopped pitted black olives

COLLEEN'S LEGENDARY SEVEN-LAYER BEAN DIP

When the slopes are conquered and the boots come off, nothing hits the spot like this epic layered bean dip. It's creamy, cheesy, and packed with flavor—just the thing to fuel those après-ski stories (and maybe a second round of chips). Back when K3 first started, the crew would gather in David and Colleen's house, rehashing the day's runs, Colleen was always there, serving up her famous layered bean dip—a nostalgic, crowd-pleasing staple that became as much a part of the routine as fresh powder and first tracks. This version stays true to those early days, delivering all the comforting flavors that fueled the adventures and good times. Here's to Colleen—and to the memories that still make us smile.

1. Preheat the oven to 375°F (190°C)—because warm, melty cheese waits for no one.

2. Mash the avocados in a bowl with the lemon juice and Tabasco until smooth and zippy. Season with a pinch of salt and pepper.

3. In a separate bowl, combine the sour cream, mayonnaise, chili powder, cumin, garlic powder, paprika, salt, and pepper. Stir until smooth.

4. Spread the refried beans in an oven-safe dish: An 8 x 8-inch (20 x 20 cm) dish works perfectly. Smooth the avocado layer on top—think creamy snowdrift. Slather on the spiced sour cream mixture like you're frosting a savory mountain.

5. Blanket everything with the cheddar and mozzarella cheeses—don't hold back. More cheese = more happiness.

6. Bake for 20 to 25 minutes, until the cheese is melted, golden, and bubbling like an après-ski hot tub.

7. Once out of the oven, sprinkle the green onions, cilantro, and black olives over the top for a fresh, colorful finish.

8. Serve warm with a mountain of tortilla chips—and watch it disappear faster than your first run of the day.

SUMMIT SOUPS

There's always a pot of soup waiting at the lodge when guests return from a day on the slopes—comfort food at its finest and the perfect way to warm up after a cat skiing adventure. Every soup I make begins with a base of onions, slowly sweated over low heat to coax out their natural sweetness without a hint of color. This gentle process builds a deep, rich foundation, giving each bowl a comforting, full-bodied flavor. Once the onions are just right, a good-quality stock takes over, and the rest of the soup comes together almost effortlessly.

"SUNSET" ROASTED BUTTERNUT SQUASH SOUP

SERVES

8

2 large butternut squash (about 4–5 lb. in total), peeled, diced, and cut into small pieces

2 large onions, chopped

6 garlic cloves, peeled

4 tbsp. (60 ml) olive oil

6 cups (1.5 L) vegetable broth (or chicken broth if preferred)

6 fresh thyme sprigs

1 cup (240 ml) heavy cream

Sea salt and freshly ground black pepper to taste

OPTIONAL GARNISH

roasted pumpkin seeds, a drizzle of olive oil or cream, and fresh herbs (thyme or parsley work well)

This golden-hued soup is as quietly essential as Denise, one of our amazing housekeepers. Roasting the squash draws out its natural sweetness, resulting in a velvety bowl of warmth that's simple, nourishing, and deeply comforting. It has the same easygoing charm as the Sunset run at K3—a mellow glide that leaves you feeling content from the inside out. Like Denise, this soup doesn't make a fuss, but it's loved by everyone and impossible to imagine the lodge without. Bonus: It's a total crowd-pleaser and a breeze to make.

1. Preheat the oven to 350°F (175°C). Line a large baking sheet with parchment paper; this is your secret weapon for an easy cleanup

2. Spread the butternut squash, onion, and garlic across the prepared baking sheet. Give them a generous toss in olive oil to coat evenly, then roast for 50 to 55 minutes, or until the butternut squash is caramelized and the onion is golden and tender. This slow roasting will give the soup its unforgettable depth of flavor.

3. Once roasted, transfer the vegetables to a large pot, making sure to scrape in all those delicious, caramelized bits from the tray—they're pure flavor gold! Pour in the broth and add the thyme. Let the pot simmer for about 20 minutes, allowing the flavors to meld into a silky, savory soup.

4. Once the soup has simmered and smells incredible, use an immersion blender to puree it until smooth. If you don't have an immersion blender, carefully blend in batches using a regular blender.

5. After blending the soup until smooth, pass it through a fine-mesh sieve into a clean pot, pressing with a spatula to extract every bit of that velvety goodness. This step ensures an ultra-silky texture that will make each spoonful incredibly luxurious.

6. Stir in the cream for an extra layer of luxury, then season with salt and pepper to taste.

7. Ladle the soup into eight warm bowls and finish each one with a drizzle of olive oil, a sprinkle of crunchy pumpkin seeds, and perhaps a few fresh herbs for a final burst of color.

WINTER PISTOU SOUP

When the snow's coming down sideways and the windows are fogged from the fire, this soup is my go-to cozy bowl. It's inspired by the soupe au pistou I fell in love with while spending time in Provence, in the sun-drenched south of France. I've given it a wintery alpine twist—chunky veggies, tender beans, and a swirl of that punchy Provençal pistou (think pesto's garlicky cousin) to brighten everything up. I've made it countless times for lodge guests, and there's something so special about watching everyone warm up with a steaming bowl in hand, cheeks still rosy from the slopes.

SERVES

6

SOUP

2 tbsp. (30 ml) olive oil

1 large onion, finely chopped

2 carrots, peeled and diced

2 garlic cloves, minced

2 medium potatoes, peeled and diced

1 zucchini, diced (or winter squash for a seasonal twist)

1 cup (150 g) green beans, trimmed and cut into 1-inch pieces

1 can (400 g) white beans (such as cannellini), drained and rinsed

1 can (400 g) diced tomatoes

6 cups (1.5 L) vegetable or chicken broth

1 bay leaf

1 fresh thyme sprig (or ½ tsp. dried thyme)

Sea salt and freshly ground black pepper to taste

PISTOU (BASIL SAUCE)

1 cup (25 g) fresh basil leaves

1 garlic clove

3 tbsp. (15 g) grated Parmesan cheese

4 tbsp. (60 ml) olive oil

Sea salt to taste

1. Heat the olive oil in a large pot over low to medium heat. Toss in the onion and carrots and sauté for about 8 to 10 minutes, until they're softened and starting to smell amazing. Add in the garlic and cook for another minute—we're building flavor here, so don't rush this step!

2. Now, the fun part—throw in those potatoes, zucchini, and green beans. Follow with the white beans, tomatoes, and broth, and stir it all up. Add the bay leaf and thyme, season with salt and pepper, and bring it all to a boil. Once it's boiling, turn down the heat and let it simmer for about 30 minutes—time for the flavors to really come together.

3. While the soup is doing its thing, it's time to whip up the pistou. In a food processor (or a mortar and pestle if you're feeling fancy), combine the basil, garlic, and Parmesan cheese. Slowly add the olive oil until it's all smooth and lush. Taste it and add a pinch of salt if needed. This is where the flavor pops!

4. Remove the bay leaf and thyme sprig from the soup. Ladle into six bowls, then swirl a big spoonful of the pistou right on top—this is where it gets extra delicious. If you're feeling fancy, sprinkle with some extra Parmesan cheese and drizzle with a bit more olive oil.

SWEET CORN AND COCONUT SOUP WITH GINGER AND LIME

SERVES

8

2 large onions, diced

1-inch (2.5 cm) piece of fresh ginger, finely grated

4 garlic cloves, minced

8 kaffir lime leaves

3 cups (450 g) sweet corn kernels (fresh, canned, or frozen)

2 cups (480 ml) coconut milk

6 cups (1.5 L) vegetable or chicken stock

Sea salt and freshly ground black pepper to taste

1 tbsp. (15 ml) freshly squeezed lime juice (to balance the sweetness)

1 tsp. (7 g) agave

Fresh cilantro to garnish

After a long day carving through fresh powder, there's nothing like wrapping your hands around a warm bowl of something comforting. That's when my Sweet Corn and Coconut Soup with Ginger and Lime makes its appearance. It's a bit of a curveball at the lodge—not your typical alpine fare. The natural sweetness of the corn, combined with the creamy coconut and zingy ginger, catches people off guard, yet they can't stop going back for more. It's like a tropical escape on a chilly winter day, and the immune-boosting ginger ensures you're ready for more adventures on the slopes.

1. Heat a large pot over medium heat and add the olive oil. While the pot is heating, prepare for the most important (and often overlooked) step—sweating the onions! Toss in the onions and cook them gently for about 20 minutes. "Sweating" is a fancy term for allowing the onions to soften slowly without browning. This technique enhances their natural sweetness, creating a rich, flavorful base for the soup.

2. Once the onions are soft and fragrant, stir in the ginger, garlic, and lime leaves. Cook for another 2 minutes, filling your kitchen with incredible aromas.

3. Add the sweet corn, stirring to coat them in the onion, garlic, and ginger goodness. Cook for 5 minutes, allowing all the flavors to mingle beautifully.

4. Pour in the stock and coconut milk, stirring everything together. Bring the soup to a gentle boil, then lower the heat to a simmer. Let it cook for about 20 to 25 minutes, or until the carrots are tender enough to blend.

5. Using an immersion blender (or a regular blender in batches), blend the soup until smooth. For an extra silky texture, pass the blended soup through a fine-mesh sieve into a clean pot to remove any leftover bits of corn skin or fiber.

6. Season with the salt, pepper, lime juice, and agave. Give it a taste—if it's too sweet, add a pinch of salt; if you want more warmth, throw in some extra ginger.

7. Ladle the soup into eight bowls and garnish with cilantro. A swirl of extra coconut milk on top adds a lovely finishing touch and makes it look extra fancy.

CREAMY MUSHROOM SOUP WITH THYME

SERVES

8

¼ cup (57 g) unsalted, butter

3 tbsp. (45 ml) olive oil

2 large onions, diced

10 cups (907 g) mixed mushrooms (such as cremini, shiitake, and button), sliced

4 garlic cloves, minced

1 cup (240 ml) dry white wine (optional, for extra depth)

6 cups (1.5 L) chicken or vegetable broth

1 fresh thyme sprig

2 cups (480 ml) whole milk or cream

Chopped fresh parsley (for garnish)

Crusty bread or croutons for serving

There's something about the earthy, rich flavor of mushrooms that makes them the perfect base for a cozy soup. This creamy wild mushroom soup, with its deep layers of flavor, always feels indulgent. The sautéed mushrooms, garlic, and fresh herbs create a savory, umami-packed broth, while the cream adds a silky texture that makes each spoonful irresistible. Packed with B vitamins and antioxidants, mushrooms are a great way to boost energy and support recovery after a day of skiing. It's a recipe I love to make, and it's always a hit with our French-Canadian guests. They tell me it reminds them of home—something about that rich, comforting flavor speaks to them, and I can't help but feel a little extra warmth when I serve it.

1. In a large pot, heat the butter and olive oil over medium-low heat. Add the onions and cook gently for 15 to 20 minutes, stirring occasionally. Allow them to sweat until they become soft and golden, developing a rich, deep flavor that will serve as the foundation for your soup.

2. Add the mushrooms to the pot and increase the heat to medium. Cook for about 10 to 15 minutes, stirring occasionally, until the mushrooms are well-browned and caramelized. This step enhances their earthy flavor, making the soup even more delicious.

3. Stir in the garlic and cook for 1 to 2 minutes until fragrant. Add the white wine (if using) and cook for 2 to 3 minutes, scraping up any browned bits from the bottom—these add rich, deep flavor.

4. Add the broth and thyme. Bring the mixture to a simmer and cook for about 15 minutes, allowing the flavors to meld together beautifully.

5. Blend the soup with an immersion blender until smooth and creamy. If using a regular blender, work in batches and blend carefully to avoid splashes.

6. For an extra silky texture, pass the blended soup through a sieve into a clean pot, removing any remaining bits for a refined finish.

7. Stir in the milk or cream and heat until just warmed through. Season with salt and pepper to taste, adjusting as needed for the perfect balance.

8. Ladle the soup into eight bowls. Top with parsley and crusty bread or croutons (optional).

ROASTED TOMATO SOUP WITH BACON AND ROSEMARY

SERVES

8

4 lb. (1.8 kg) ripe tomatoes (Roma or plum work well), halved

2 tbsp. (30 ml) olive oil

Sea salt and freshly ground black pepper to taste

6 slices thick-cut bacon

2 large onions, diced

6 garlic cloves, minced

1 tbsp. (2 g) finely chopped fresh rosemary

2 tbsp. (35 g) tomato paste

6 cups (1.5 L) chicken or vegetable broth

1 tbsp. (15 ml) balsamic vinegar (for added depth)

½ cup (120 ml) heavy cream

Fresh rosemary sprigs (for garnish)

Crusty bread for serving (to soak up that smoky goodness!)

This isn't just any tomato soup—roasting the tomatoes deepens their natural sweetness, while the fresh rosemary brings a wonderfully earthy, piney note that makes you feel like you're still breathing in the fresh alpine air. And then, of course, there's the bacon! Those crispy, smoky bits bring the whole dish together, adding an indulgent touch that every skier craves after a day carving through powder. As much as I love a classic tomato soup, there's always room for another variation, and this one has become a go-to favorite at the lodge.

1 Preheat the oven to 400°F (200°C). Place the halved tomatoes cut side up on a baking sheet. Drizzle with the olive oil and season with salt and pepper. Roast for 35 to 40 minutes, until the tomatoes are soft, slightly caramelized, and bursting with sweetness.

2 In a large pot, cook the bacon over medium heat until crispy, about 5 to 7 minutes. Remove the bacon and set aside on paper towels to drain. Keep the bacon fat in the pot—you'll use it to cook the onions for extra flavor!

3 In the same pot, add the onions and sweat for 20 minutes in the bacon fat over low heat, stirring occasionally, until softened and golden. This slow process will intensify the flavor of the soup.

4 Add the garlic and rosemary to the onions, cooking for another 2 minutes until fragrant. The aroma at this point will be incredible!

5 Stir in the tomato paste and cook for 1 to 2 minutes. Add the tomatoes to the pot, along with the chicken or vegetable broth. Bring to a simmer and let it cook for 20 minutes, allowing the flavors to meld together.

6 Using an immersion blender (or transferring in batches to a blender), blend the soup until smooth. After blending, pass the soup through a fine mesh sieve into a clean pot, pressing down with a spoon to remove the tomato seeds and skins. This step not only gives the soup a velvety texture but also eliminates any seeds that could make the soup bitter. Be careful when blending hot liquids.

7 Stir in the balsamic vinegar for an extra layer of flavor, then add the cream and stir until the soup is creamy and smooth. Season with salt and pepper to taste. Give it one last taste check—balance the flavors to your liking!

8 Ladle the soup into eight bowls and crumble the crispy bacon on top of each serving. Garnish with rosemary sprigs for an aromatic touch. Serve with crusty bread for dipping.

SWEET POTATO, LEEK, AND LENTIL SOUP

SERVES

8

2 large, sweet potatoes, peeled and diced

2 leeks, trimmed, cleaned, and sliced (white and light green parts only)

2 tbsp. (30 ml) olive oil

2 large onions, diced

3 garlic cloves, minced

1 + ½ cups (285 g) red lentils, rinsed

2 tsp. dried thyme (or 4 fresh thyme sprigs)

8 cups (1.5 L) vegetable or chicken broth

Sea salt and freshly ground black pepper to taste

1 cup (240 ml) coconut milk or heavy cream

Fresh thyme or parsley (for garnish)

Crusty bread for serving (to soak up every drop!)

This soup is the perfect blend of earthy flavors and cozy comfort. Sweet potatoes bring their natural sweetness and creamy texture, while the lentils add protein to refuel those tired legs. The leeks are the unsung hero of this soup, adding a subtle depth, and thyme gives it that irresistible wintery aroma. This soup is easy to whip up but tastes like you have spent hours crafting the perfect après-ski meal. This soup came to life when the dry stores were running low. I tossed in some lentils to stretch things out and thicken the soup. And it turned out to be an unexpected hit.

1. Slice up those sweet potatoes into bite-size chunks and give the leeks a good rinse, then slice. If you've got ski gloves on, take them off first—trust me!

2. In a large pot, heat the olive oil over medium-low heat. Add the onions and let them cook gently for 15 to 20 minutes, stirring occasionally, until they're golden and sweet. This slow sweating process gives the soup a deep, rich flavor base.

3. Once the onions are golden, add the leeks and garlic to the pot, cooking for another 5 minutes until softened.

4. Stir in the sweet potatoes, lentils, and thyme. Let them soak up the flavors in the pot for about 2 minutes. This step helps the ingredients blend before the liquid is added.

5. Pour in the vegetable or chicken broth and bring the soup to a boil. Then reduce the heat to low, cover, and simmer for 25 to 30 minutes, or until the lentils and sweet potatoes are soft and tender. Time to sit by the fire and relax while the magic happens!

6. If you like your soup smooth and silky, use an immersion blender for a quick blend (or transfer in batches to a blender). Prefer it chunky? Skip this step for a rustic texture or blend just half for the best of both worlds.

7. Stir in the coconut milk or cream for extra creaminess and season with salt and pepper to taste.

8. Ladle the soup into eight bowls and garnish with thyme or parsley for a pop of color. Serve with crusty bread on the side.

SERVES

8

4 tbsp. (60 ml) olive oil

2 large onions, diced

3 garlic cloves, minced

1 tsp. fennel seeds (for a hint of anise flavor)

2 small heads of cauliflower, broken into florets

½ large, sweet potato, peeled and diced (for color and light sweetness)

8 cups (1.5 L) vegetable or chicken broth

2 tsp. (10 g) freshly squeezed lemon juice (brightens up the flavors)

Sea salt and freshly ground black pepper to taste

Fresh parsley or fennel fronds (for garnish)

Crusty bread for serving (because you'll want to mop up every bit!)

CAULIFLOWER, FENNEL, AND SWEET POTATO SOUP

Cauliflower is one of those wonderfully versatile veggies I always reach for when I want something comforting but not too heavy. It plays well with bold flavors and gentle ones alike, and in this soup, it's pure magic. The creamy, nutty flavor of cauliflower mingles perfectly with the subtle anise kick of fennel seeds, while a hint of sweet potato adds a lovely blush and a touch of warmth. Slowly cooked onions bring a gentle sweetness that gives this soup that extra something special.

1. In a big soup pot, heat the olive oil over low to medium-low heat. Toss in the onions and let them cook slowly, stirring every now and then. We're talking 20 minutes here, while they soften, turn golden, and develop a deliciously sweet, caramelized magic. Taking the time to caramelize the onions will give the soup a delicious depth and balance the flavors beautifully!

2. Once those onions are soft and sweet, add the garlic and fennel seeds. Stir and let them cook for another minute or two until the whole kitchen smells amazing

3. Toss in the cauliflower and sweet potato. Give everything a good stir to coat with the caramelized goodness. Let the veggies soften for about 5 minutes, warming them up for their big soup debut.

4. Pour in the broth, crank up the heat until it starts to bubble, then lower it and cover. Let it simmer for 25 to 30 minutes, or until the cauliflower and sweet potato are soft enough to blend. Check the pot occasionally—the aroma should be irresistible by now.

5. Use an immersion blender to transform everything into a creamy, dreamy soup with that perfect blush color. (No immersion blender? Just work in batches with a regular blender—careful, it's hot! —and return the soup to the pot.)

6. Stir in the lemon juice to give the soup a little zing. Taste and add salt and pepper as needed to balance everything out.

7. Ladle into eight bowls, garnish with parsley or fennel fronds, and serve with crusty bread.

FELIX'S FRENCH ONION SOUP

SERVES

4–6

SOUP

3 tbsp. (43 g) unsalted butter

2 tbsp. (30 ml) olive oil

5 large yellow onions (about 1.25 kg), thinly sliced

1 tsp. sugar
(for deeper caramelization)

3 garlic cloves, minced

1 tbsp. (15 g) all-purpose flour
(for a little thickness)

1 cup (240 ml) dry white wine
(or dry sherry for a richer twist)

6 cups (1.5 L) beef broth
(or a mix of beef and chicken broth for more balance)

2 bay leaves

4 fresh thyme sprigs
(or 1 tsp. dried thyme)

1 tsp. (5 g) Worcestershire sauce

Sea salt and freshly ground black pepper to taste

CHEESY TOAST

6 slices of baguette (about 1-inch-thick sturdy enough for dunking!)

1 + ½ cups (150 g) grated Gruyère cheese (or a mix of Gruyère and Comté)

3 tbsp. (45 g) Parmesan cheese
(optional, for extra savory bite)

When the snow's piling up and the air is crisp, nothing hits the spot like a bowl of rich, cheesy French onion soup. This one's for Felix, our favorite French Canadian tail guide, known as the "Swiss Army knife of K3" with his jokes, French humor, and fearless approach to skiing. With slow-caramelized onions, savory broth, and gooey melted cheese, this soup is like wrapping yourself in a warm, melty blanket. While Felix didn't invent the recipe, it's got all the comforting, cozy vibes of a true French-Canadian classic—always a crowd favorite, just like his straight-line descents and those unforgettable days on the mountain.

1. In a large heavy-bottomed pot, melt the butter with the olive oil over medium heat. Toss in the onions with a pinch of salt and cook, stirring occasionally, until they turn a deep golden brown—about 45 minutes. Want to speed things up a bit? Add the sugar halfway through to help with caramelization—but patience pays off here!

2. Stir in the garlic and cook for 1 minute. Sprinkle in the flour and stir until the onions are nicely coated—this helps thicken the broth just a touch. Pour in the white wine and scrape up all those caramelized bits from the bottom of the pot (flavor gold!). Simmer for 5 minutes to let the wine reduce.

3. Add the beef broth, bay leaves, thyme, and Worcestershire sauce. Bring it to a simmer, lower the heat, and let it bubble gently for 30 minutes—the longer it simmers, the cozier it tastes. Season with salt and pepper to taste, then remove the herbs.

4. Preheat the broiler (or oven grill) to high. Arrange the baguette slices on a baking sheet and toast both sides until crisp—about 2 minutes per side. Pile each slice with a generous handful of Gruyère cheese (and a sprinkle of Parmesan cheese if you're feeling fancy), then broil until bubbling and golden.

5. Ladle the hot soup into four to six oven-safe bowls. Top each with a cheese-topped baguette and broil for 2 to 3 minutes until golden and melted. For packed lunches, keep the toasts separate and dunk when ready.

6. Serve immediately, with extra cheesy baguette slices on the side—because no one ever says no to more cheese. It's hearty, comforting, and guaranteed to bring everyone back for seconds after a chilly day on the slopes.

"ANARCHY" BROCCOLI AND CHEDDAR SOUP

SERVES

8

3 tbsp. (45 ml) olive oil

2 large onions, finely chopped

4 garlic cloves, minced

6 cups broccoli florets (about 3 large heads)

1 tsp. (1 g) fresh thyme

6 cups (1.4 L) vegetable or chicken stock

1 handful fresh spinach (for color)

2 cups (480 ml) whole milk or cream (for added creaminess)

4 cups (454 g) shredded sharp cheddar cheese

Sea salt and a grind of freshly ground black pepper

Inspired by the chaos of the legendary Anarchy run at K3, this broccoli and cheddar soup is the ultimate post-run reward: hearty, comforting, and loaded with flavor. The earthy broccoli meets sharp cheddar cheese in a combo as bold as your K3 descent, with a sneaky handful of spinach tossed in for color. Whether you rode the Anarchy run like a hero or made it down with a grin and a few face-plants, this soup is your well-deserved edible pat on the back.

1. In a large pot, heat the olive oil over low heat. Add the onions and cook gently for 15 to 20 minutes, stirring occasionally. This low and slow method draws out their natural sweetness. Once the onions are golden and softened, add the garlic and cook for another 1 to 2 minutes until fragrant.

2. Add the broccoli and thyme to the pot, pour in the broth, and bring everything to a simmer. Cover and cook for 10 to 15 minutes, or until the broccoli is tender. In the last 2 minutes of cooking, add the spinach; it will wilt quickly and brighten the soup with a vibrant green color.

3. Using an immersion blender, blend the soup until smooth (or transfer in batches to a blender). For a perfectly smooth texture, pass the blended soup through a sieve to remove any fibrous bits from the broccoli and spinach.

4. Finally, stir in the milk or cream, followed by the cheddar cheese. Allow the cheese to melt into the soup, stirring until it is smooth and creamy.

5. Season with salt and pepper as needed for balance.

SKI LODGE SALADS

Salads are often the unsung heroes of a meal—quietly packed with vitamins, enzymes, and everything your body needs, yet too often dismissed as bland or boring. Not here. At the lodge, we kick off every dinner service with a vibrant salad. After a round of hearty après-ski appetizers, a crisp, refreshing plate is the perfect palate reset before the main course. Each salad is built with the freshest organic vegetables we can find, and every dressing is crafted to be as fun, flavorful, and memorable as the mountain day that came before it.

When preparing these salads at home, you've got two great serving options: go casual and serve them straight from the bowl for a communal help-yourself vibe—or take the elegant route and plate them individually, layering the ingredients for a more refined presentation.

CRISP ALPINE SALAD WITH BACON AND FETA WITH AVOCADO RANCH DRESSING

SERVES
4

AVOCADO RANCH DRESSING

1 whole ripe avocado

1 cup (240 ml) buttermilk

½ cup (120 ml) sour cream

1 garlic clove, grated

2 tsp. (10 g) freshly squeezed lemon juice

2 tbsp. (30 ml) extra-virgin olive oil

½ tsp. (2.5g) salt

4 tbsp. (8-12 g) fresh chopped herbs (Italian parsley, dill, chives)

SALAD

8 slices bacon, cooked until crispy and crumbled

½ cup (60 g) pecans, toasted and roughly chopped

8 oz. (225 g) baby spinach, washed and dried

1 head romaine lettuce, chopped

1 cup (100 g) crumbled feta cheese

1 cup (150 g) cherry tomatoes, halved

1 red onion, thinly sliced (optional)

1 apple, cored and thinly sliced (Granny Smith or Honeycrisp work well)

A salad as bold as your backcountry bragging rights, this leafy legend delivers serious crunch with romaine and spinach, a smoky hit from crispy bacon bits, and just the right zing from sharp crumbled feta. And let's talk about that Avocado Ranch Dressing—I love using avocado because it's not just delicious, it's packed with healthy fats that do your body some good. Creamy, nourishing, and smoother than your line through untouched pow (at least in your head), this salad is fresh, hearty, and worthy of your off-piste adventures. Salad, but make it extreme.

1. Slice the ripe avocado in half, remove the pit, and scoop the flesh into a blender or food processor. Alternatively, mash the avocado with a fork until very smooth.

2. Now add the buttermilk, sour cream, garlic, lemon juice, olive oil, and salt to the blender with the avocado. Blend until smooth and creamy, scraping down the sides as needed.

3. Toss in the herbs and pulse briefly. Aim for a textured dressing with visible flecks of herbs for extra flavor and visual appeal.

4. Taste the dressing and adjust the seasoning, adding more salt or lemon juice if desired. Transfer it to a jar or bowl. Use immediately or store in the refrigerator for up to 3 days. Stir before serving, as the dressing may thicken slightly.

5. In a skillet over medium heat, cook the bacon until crispy. Transfer to a paper towel–lined plate to drain, then crumble once cooled.

6. In a dry skillet over medium heat, toast the pecans for 3 to 5 minutes, stirring frequently until fragrant and lightly golden.

7. Layer the baby spinach and romaine in a large bowl as the base. Next, arrange the feta cheese, bacon, cherry tomatoes, red onion, apple, and pecans in layers over the greens, creating a colorful, visually appealing display. To assemble on individual plates, layer each ingredient separately on each of the four dishes.

8. Finish with a delicate pour of the Avocado Ranch Dressing just before serving.

MEDITERRANEAN ROASTED VEGETABLE SALAD WITH TAHINI DRESSING

SERVES
4

TAHINI DRESSING

3 tbsp. (45 ml) tahini

1 tbsp. (15 ml) freshly squeezed lemon juice

1 garlic clove, minced

1 tsp. (7 g) maple syrup or honey

2–3 tbsp. water (to thin, if needed)

2 tbsp. (30 ml) olive oil

Sea salt and freshly ground black pepper to taste

SALAD

2 medium sweet potatoes, peeled and cubed

1 tbsp. (15 g) olive oil

Sea salt and freshly ground pepper

1 red pepper

8 oz. (225 g) mixed salad leaves (such as arugula, spinach, and romaine)

½ cup (75 g) black olives, pitted and halved

¼ cup (70 g) chopped sun-dried tomatoes

¼ cup (30 g) flaked almonds, toasted

½ cup (75 g) chopped dried apricots

¼ cup (12 g) fresh basil leaves, torn

2 tbsp. finely chopped fresh parsley

This Mediterranean-inspired salad is my idea of the perfect first course—bursting with sunshine and goodness to revive your spirits. Years of being a yacht chef sailing through the Med have left their mark on my cooking, and I love bringing those sun-drenched flavors to the mountains. Roasted sweet potatoes and smoky red peppers add a bit of coastal magic to your chilly alpine retreat, while zesty sun-dried tomatoes, briny black olives, and a scattering of fresh herbs bring that unmistakable Mediterranean soul. And the real star? The creamy Tahini Dressing—nutty, rich, and velvety—that ties it all together like the perfect sun-kissed soundtrack.

1. In a small bowl, combine the tahini, lemon juice, garlic, and maple syrup or honey. Whisk it all together. Gradually add water, a tablespoon at a time, until you achieve a creamy, pourable consistency. Now drizzle in the olive oil and mix until it's all harmoniously blended. This will give your dressing that delightful richness we all crave! Adjust the seasoning and set aside.

2. Preheat the oven to 400°F (200°C). Toss the sweet potato cubes with a little olive oil, salt, and pepper. Spread them on a baking sheet and roast for 20 to 25 minutes, or until golden and tender. Let cool slightly.

3. Preheat the oven to 450°F (230°C). Place the whole red pepper on a foil-lined baking sheet. Roast for 20 to 25 minutes, turning occasionally, until the skin is charred and the pepper is soft. Transfer the pepper to a bowl, cover with plastic wrap, and let steam for 10 minutes. This helps loosen the skin. Peel off the skin, remove the stems and seeds, and slice the pepper into strips.

4. Arrange the mixed salad leaves on a large serving platter or divide them among four individual plates. Layer on the sweet potatoes, black olives, red pepper strips, sun-dried tomatoes, dried apricots, almonds, basil, and parsley. Drizzle the Tahini Dressing over the salad just before serving to preserve its vibrant colors and freshness.

SERVES

4

GREEN GODDESS DRESSING

½ cup (15 g) fresh parsley

½ cup (10 g) fresh cilantro

½ ripe avocado

½ cup (120 g) plain Greek yogurt or sour cream

¼ cup (60 g) mayonnaise

2 tbsp. (30 ml) freshly squeezed lemon juice

1 garlic clove, minced

2 scallions, chopped (green and white parts)

Sea salt and freshly ground black pepper to taste

Water, as needed to adjust consistency

Drizzle of extra-virgin olive oil (about 2 tbsp. or to taste)

SALAD

1 lb. (450 g) assorted salad greens

1 medium cucumber, shaved into ribbons

1 ripe avocado, diced

1 cup (150 g) cherry tomatoes, halved

1 cup (90 g) broccoli florets, chopped into bite-size pieces

2 tbsp. (6 g) chopped chives

¼ cup (30 g) pumpkin seeds (pepitas)

Sea salt and freshly ground black pepper to taste

GARDEN GREENS SALAD WITH VERDANT GODDESS DRESSING

I've always had a soft spot for green ingredients, and this salad is my go-to when I want something fresh, colorful, and energizing. With a dynamic mix of crisp greens, crunchy cucumbers, and a rainbow of vegetables, every bite is a little burst of joy. And the real magic? Our Verdant Goddess Dressing—a creamy, herb-packed dream that ties it all together with a zesty kick. Whether you're enjoying it as a light lunch or a side to your favorite lodge meal, this salad is as refreshing and satisfying as a deep breath of mountain air.

1. Make the dressing first. In a blender or food processor, add the parsley and cilantro. Scoop in the half avocado for a creamy texture, followed by the Greek yogurt or sour cream and mayonnaise. This is where the richness comes from!

2. Pour in the lemon juice, toss in the garlic, and add the scallions. Blend everything until smooth and creamy. If it's too thick for your liking, add a splash of water to achieve your desired consistency. Once blended, drizzle in the olive oil while the blender is running.

3. Now to prepare the greens: In a large salad bowl, add the mixed greens as the base for your colorful salad. Layer in the cucumber, avocado, cherry tomatoes, and broccoli.

4. Sprinkle the chives and pumpkin seeds over the top. Add salt and pepper to taste. For a more elegant option, divide the salad onto four individual plates, layering each ingredient separately.

5. Drizzle the dressing over the salad just before serving.

SERVES

4

VINAIGRETTE

1 cup (240 ml) freshly squeezed orange juice

Zest of 1 orange, minced

1 shallot, minced

2 tbsp. (30 ml) white wine vinegar

½ tsp. (2.5 g) sea salt

½ cup (120 ml) olive oil

SALAD

1 lb. (450 g) mixed greens (such as arugula, spinach, or a spring mix)

2 ripe pears, thinly sliced (Bartlett or Bosc work well)

½ cup (75 g) crumbled blue cheese

½ cup (60 g) walnuts, toasted and roughly chopped

¼ cup (70 g) dried cranberries or pomegranate seeds

PEAR AND BLUE CHEESE SALAD WITH ORANGE VINAIGRETTE

This salad brings the bold with creamy blue cheese, the sweet with juicy pears, and the crunch with toasted walnuts. But for me, it's always about the dressing. I love crafting dressings that bring a salad to life, and this Orange Vinaigrette is one of my favorites—zesty, bright, and versatile enough to shine on all sorts of greens and combos. Elegant, refreshing, and just indulgent enough to feel like a reward—this is alpine chic dining, even if you're still defrosting your fingers.

1. Pour the orange juice into a small saucepan and bring it to a gentle simmer over medium heat. Allow it to simmer until it reduces by half, which should take about 10 to 15 minutes. Stir occasionally to prevent sticking. You should end up with about ½ cup (120 ml) of concentrated orange juice. Allow to cool slightly.

2. In a mixing bowl, whisk together the reduced orange juice, orange zest, shallot, white wine vinegar, and salt. Slowly drizzle in the olive oil while continuously whisking to emulsify the vinaigrette. Adjust seasoning and set aside.

3. In a large salad bowl, layer the mixed greens as the base. Layer the pears on top for a beautiful presentation. Sprinkle the blue cheese evenly over the pears. Add the walnuts for a delightful crunch and scatter the dried cranberries or pomegranate seeds for sweetness and color.

4. Drizzle with the Orange Vinaigrette just before serving or serve the dressing on the side.

SUNBURST LAYERED SALAD WITH GARLIC CITRUS PARSLEY DRESSING

SERVES

4

GARLIC CITRUS PARSLEY DRESSING

¼ cup (60 ml) olive oil

2 tbsp. (30 ml) freshly squeezed lemon juice

1 tbsp. (15 ml) freshly squeezed orange juice

1 garlic clove, minced

2 tbsp. (30 g) chopped fresh parsley

½ tsp. (2.5 g) sea salt (adjust to taste)

¼ tsp. ground black pepper (adjust to taste)

SALAD

1 head romaine lettuce, chopped

8 oz. (225 g) fresh baby spinach

2 cups (220 g) grated carrots

1 apple, cored and sliced (preferably a sweet variety like Fuji or Honeycrisp)

½ cup (80 g) raisins

¼ cup (32 g) pumpkin seeds

½ small red onion, thinly sliced

1 cup (113 g) sharp cheddar cheese, diced

Embrace the spirit of the slopes with this invigorating "Sunshine Salad"—a dish born from a bit of lodge-side creativity. One snowy morning, the lettuce arrived looking a little tired (as it sometimes does after its long journey up the mountain), so I had to stretch the two heads of romaine I had left. The result? A vibrant, crunchy medley of grated carrots, crisp romaine, juicy apple slices, and sharp cheddar cheese—bright, bold, and totally satisfying.

A handful of fresh spinach and sweet raisins adds earthy depth and natural sweetness, while the zesty Garlic Citrus Parsley Dressing brings it all together with a refreshing kick. Nutritious, full of flavor, and bursting with personality, this salad quickly became a winter favorite—and a testament to how even a dish born out of necessity can turn into something truly delicious.

1. In a blender, combine the olive oil, lemon juice, orange juice, garlic, parsley, salt, and pepper. Blend on high until smooth and well combined, about 15 to 30 seconds. Taste and adjust the seasoning as needed.

2. In a large bowl or on four individual plates, begin with a base of romaine lettuce. Add a layer of baby spinach, then scatter the carrots evenly over the greens. Arrange the apple slices on top, fanning them out for a touch of elegance. Sprinkle over the raisins for sweetness and the pumpkin seeds for a satisfying crunch. Add thin slices of red onion for a zesty kick. Just before serving, drizzle the Garlic Citrus Parsley Dressing generously over the salad. Finish with a sprinkle of diced sharp cheddar cheese for a creamy, tangy touch.

3. Serve immediately to preserve its fresh and crisp texture.

SERVES

4

BASIL DRESSING

1 cup (20 g) fresh basil leaves

¼ cup (60 ml) extra-virgin olive oil

2 tbsp. (30 ml) balsamic vinegar

1 tbsp. (15 ml) honey or maple syrup

1 garlic clove, minced

1 tbsp. (15 g) Dijon mustard

Sea salt and freshly ground black pepper to taste

SALAD

1 lb. (450 g) mixed greens (arugula, spinach, and romaine)

1 cup (150 g) cherry tomatoes, halved

1 red bell pepper, diced

1 cup (120 g) diced cucumber

1 cup (115 g) radishes, thinly sliced

½ cup (40 g) shredded red cabbage

2 scallions, finely chopped

1 avocado, diced

½ cup (60 g) crumbled goat's cheese

¼ cup (30 g) walnuts, chopped, for extra crunch

COLORFUL CRUNCH SALAD WITH GOAT CHEESE AND BASIL DRESSING

A dazzling array of colorful veggies, as varied as the ski runs outside, is tossed with creamy, tangy goat cheese. It's the ideal balance of flavors and textures to revive your muscles (and your sense of adventure) after charging the backcountry. Each bite is like a burst of fresh energy, getting you prepped for your next epic run. And that house-made Basil Dressing? It's so good, I get asked for this recipe all the time! The basil is inspired by the time I've spent in Italy, and trust me, it's a favorite. Light, refreshing, and the ultimate fuel to keep you going.

1. In a blender or food processor, combine the basil leaves, olive oil, balsamic vinegar, honey or maple syrup, garlic, Dijon mustard, salt, and pepper. Blend until smooth and creamy. Taste and adjust seasoning as needed. Set aside.

2. In a large salad bowl or on four individual plates, start by layering the ingredients for a stunning presentation. Begin with the mixed greens as the base on each plate. Next, layer on the cherry tomatoes for a juicy burst of flavor. Add the red bell pepper on top for a sweet crunch. Follow with the cucumber for a refreshing touch. Next, layer the radishes for a peppery bite. Add the red cabbage for color and texture. Sprinkle the scallions over the cabbage. Layer on the avocado for creaminess. Finish with the goat cheese and a sprinkle of walnuts for extra crunch.

3. Drizzle the Basil Dressing over each individual salad just before serving or serve it on the side for guests to add their desired amount.

SERVES

4

MAPLE LEMON DRESSING

3 tbsp. (45 ml) pure maple syrup

2 tbsp. (30 ml) freshly squeezed lemon juice

1 tbsp. (15 g) Dijon mustard

1 garlic clove, finely minced

¼ cup (60 ml) extra-virgin olive oil

Sea salt and freshly ground black pepper to taste

SALAD

1 lb. (450 g) mixed salad leaves (arugula, baby spinach, romaine)

2 cups (300 g) cubed butternut squash, roasted

1 crisp apple, thinly sliced (like Honeycrisp or Fuji)

½ cup (60 g) pecans, toasted

½ cup (75 g) cherry tomatoes, halved

¼ cup (30 g) dried cranberries

⅓ cup (40 g) sharp white cheddar cheese, cut into small cubes

HARVEST SALAD WITH MAPLE LEMON DRESSING

For me, this is the perfect Canadian lodge salad—packed with the autumn ingredients I grew up loving: sweet, crunchy apples, roasted butternut squash that practically melts in your mouth, and toasty pecans for that irresistible nutty warmth, all layered over crisp mixed greens. I drizzle it with a zesty Maple Lemon Dressing that ties everything together like a favorite flannel shirt—bright, comforting, and just the right amount of sweet.

1. In a small bowl, whisk together the maple syrup, lemon juice, Dijon mustard, and garlic until smooth. Slowly drizzle in the olive oil while whisking to create a creamy, well-emulsified dressing. Season with salt and pepper to taste, adjusting the sweetness or tang as desired. Set aside.

2. Preheat the oven to 400°F (200°C). Toss the squash cubes with a bit of olive oil, salt, and pepper, then spread them on a baking sheet. Roast for 20 to 25 minutes, until tender and caramelized. Set aside to cool slightly.

3. Layer the mixed greens at the bottom of a large bowl. For a more refined presentation, prepare each plate individually. Add the butternut squash, apple slices, pecans, cherry tomatoes, and dried cranberries, arranging them artfully on top.

4. Drizzle the Maple Lemon Dressing over the salad, allowing the vibrant layers shine through, then finish by sprinkling the cheddar cheese on top just before serving.

SERVES

4

SALAD

8 slices prosciutto

2 heads romaine lettuce, chopped

1 bunch arugula, washed and dried

1 cup (40 g) homemade or store-bought croutons

½ cup (50 g) grated Parmesan cheese

CREAMY CLASSIC DRESSING

¼ cup (60 g) mayonnaise

2 tbsp. (30 g) Greek yogurt

2 tbsp. (30 g) Dijon mustard

2 tbsp. (30 ml) freshly squeezed lemon juice

1 tbsp. (15 ml) olive oil

1–2 garlic cloves, minced or grated

1 tsp. (5 g) Worcestershire sauce

½ cup (50 g) grated Parmesan cheese

Sea salt and freshly ground black pepper to taste

CAESAR SALAD WITH FRAZZLED PROSCIUTTO AND CREAMY CLASSIC DRESSING

Elevate your salad game with this refreshing twist on a classic Caesar. I love adding peppery arugula to break up the romaine—it adds vibrant color and a bold, fresh flavor that really lifts the dish. Toss in some crispy, savory frazzled prosciutto, and suddenly the traditional Caesar gets a whole new personality.

1. Preheat the oven to 400°F (200°C). Arrange the prosciutto slices on a baking sheet lined with parchment paper. Bake for about 10 to 12 minutes, or until crispy. Remove from the oven and let cool. Once cooled, crumble or break into pieces.

2. In a bowl, combine the mayonnaise, yogurt, Dijon mustard, lemon juice, olive oil, garlic, Worcestershire sauce, and Parmesan cheese. Whisk until smooth and creamy. Season with salt and pepper to taste.

3. Combine the romaine and arugula in a large salad bowl. Drizzle the Caesar dressing over the greens and toss gently to combine. Add the croutons and toss lightly again to distribute. Finally, crumble the frazzled prosciutto on top of the salad and sprinkle with additional Parmesan cheese. This method allows the flavors to meld while keeping the prosciutto crispy on top. Serve immediately.

SKI LODGE SALADS

SERVES

4

HONEY BALSAMIC VINAIGRETTE

1 garlic clove, minced

1 + ½ tbsp. (22 ml) balsamic vinegar

2 tsp. (10 g) red wine vinegar

1 tbsp. (15 ml) honey

¼ tsp. (1.2 g) sea salt

¼ tsp. (.5 g) cracked black pepper

⅓ cup (80 ml) extra-virgin olive oil

SALAD

1 cup (150 g) cherry tomatoes, halved

2 tbsp. (30 ml) olive oil

Sea salt and freshly ground black pepper to taste

8 oz. (225 g) baby spinach, washed and dried

1 bunch arugula, washed and dried

2 balls (about 250 g) burrata cheese

¼ cup (100 g) toasted pine nuts

Fresh herbs such as basil or parsley (for garnish, optional)

ROASTED TOMATO SALAD WITH BURRATA AND HONEY BALSAMIC VINAIGRETTE

This is my twist on a classic spinach and tomato salad—elevated with a few cozy, lodge-worthy upgrades. A vibrant base of tender baby spinach and peppery arugula sets the stage, layered with creamy burrata and sweet, caramelized roasted cherry tomatoes. It's the kind of salad that feels a little indulgent yet wonderfully light, just what you crave after a day carving turns or chasing powder. A final drizzle of tangy Honey Balsamic Vinaigrette brings everything together.

1. In a small bowl, combine the garlic, balsamic vinegar, red wine vinegar, honey, salt, and pepper. Whisk until the ingredients are well blended. Gradually drizzle in the olive oil, whisking constantly until the vinaigrette thickens. Set aside.

2. Preheat the oven to 400°F (200°C). Place the cherry tomatoes on a baking sheet and drizzle with the olive oil. Sprinkle with salt and pepper. Roast for 10 minutes, or until the tomatoes soften and begin to caramelize around the edges. Remove from the oven and allow them to cool slightly.

3. In a large salad bowl, add the arugula and baby spinach and toss gently to combine. Add the cherry tomatoes to the greens.

4. Drizzle the Honey Balsamic Vinaigrette over the salad and toss gently to coat. Tear the burrata into pieces and arrange it on top of the salad. Sprinkle with the pine nuts for added crunch and flavor, and garnish with herbs (if using).

5. Serve immediately.

MAINS TO MELT THE SNOW

When the cold bites and the powder piles high, nothing hits the spot like a hearty main to warm you from the inside out. These are the dishes that fuel long days on the mountain and melt away the chill with every bite. Comforting, satisfying, and packed with flavor—mains that turn frostbite into fond memories. Time to dig in and refuel!

SERVES

4

CHICKEN PIE

1 whole chicken (3–4 lb.)

2 large carrots,
peeled and cut into chunks

4 bay leaves

2 fresh thyme sprigs

2 garlic cloves, smashed

1 large onion

6 cups (1.5 L) water
(or chicken stock for more flavor)

1 cup (240 ml) white wine

Sea salt and freshly ground black
pepper to taste

VELOUTÉ SAUCE

2 tbsp. (28 g) unsalted butter

2 tbsp. (15 g) all-purpose flour

2 cups (480 ml) reduced chicken stock
(from boiling the chicken)

Sea salt and freshly ground black
pepper to taste

A splash of cream,
for extra richness

PHYLLO PASTRY

4 sheets phyllo pastry

2 tbsp. (30 ml) melted butter,
for brushing

DECONSTRUCTED CHICKEN PIE WITH CRISPY PHYLLO PASTRY

One of my English clients, whom I had the pleasure of working with on his yacht in the Mediterranean, used to request a traditional chicken pie every time he visited—craving that nostalgic, comforting dish from home. This is my playful take on his favorite. Instead of the classic enclosed crust, I've gone for a golden, crispy layer of phyllo pastry that adds a light, flaky crunch to every bite—keeping things a little easier, a little lighter, but just as satisfying. Inside, you'll still find all the comforting goodness: tender chicken, savory vegetables, and a rich, creamy sauce that wraps you up like a warm blanket.

1. In a large pot, add the whole chicken, carrots, bay leaves, thyme, garlic, and onion. Pour in the water (or chicken stock) and white wine (if you're using it). Season generously with salt and pepper. Bring the pot to a boil over medium-high heat, then reduce the heat to a simmer. Let it cook for 60 to 75 minutes, or until the chicken is fully cooked and tender. You'll know it's ready when the chicken is falling off the bone and the broth smells heavenly.

2. Using tongs, remove the chicken from the pot and set it aside to cool on a plate. Carefully scoop out the carrots and set them aside for later. Discard the bay leaves, thyme, and onion, then strain the broth through a sieve back into the pot to remove any solids.

3. Simmer the broth over medium heat until it reduces to about 2 cups. This will concentrate the flavors for the sauce. Once reduced, set the broth aside.

4. Once the chicken is cool enough to handle, shred it into bite-size pieces, discarding any bones. Take the reserved carrots and chop them into small bite-size chunks.

5. In a saucepan, melt the butter over medium heat. Sprinkle in the flour and whisk continuously for 1 to 2 minutes to form a pale, smooth roux. Gradually pour in the reduced broth while whisking to prevent lumps. Let it simmer for 5 to 7 minutes until the sauce thickens to a velvety consistency. Season the sauce with salt and pepper to taste. For extra richness, add a splash of cream and stir to combine.

6   Preheat the oven to 375°F (190°C). Lay out the phyllo sheets on a clean surface, then scrunch each sheet loosely into a ball shape. Place each scrunched sheet on a baking tray. Brush each phyllo scrunch generously with melted butter. Bake for 10 to 12 minutes, or until the pastry is golden brown, crispy, and irresistible. It'll puff up and crisp up to perfection.

7   In a large bowl, combine the chicken, carrots, and a generous amount of the velouté sauce. Stir to coat the chicken and carrots in the sauce, adding more sauce if needed. Transfer the chicken mixture to a saucepan and warm over low heat, stirring occasionally until heated through.

8   Spoon the warm chicken mixture into four individual serving bowls. Gently place a crispy phyllo scrunch on top of each bowl, adding a delightful crunch to each serving.

SERVES

4

HALIBUT

4 halibut fillets,
about 6 oz. (170 g) each

Sea salt and freshly ground black pepper to taste

2 tbsp. (30 ml) olive oil (for searing)

1 cup (90 g) grated Parmesan cheese

½ cup (25 g) panko breadcrumbs

1 tbsp. (6 g) finely chopped parsley leaves

LEMON THYME CREAM SAUCE

2 tbsp. (28 g) unsalted butter

2 garlic cloves, minced

½ cup (120 ml) dry white wine

1 cup (240 ml) heavy cream

Zest of 1 lemon

2 tbsp. (30 ml) freshly squeezed lemon juice

1 tbsp. (3 g) fresh thyme leaves

Sea salt and freshly ground black pepper to taste

PARMESAN CRUSTED HALIBUT WITH LEMON THYME SAUCE

I cook a lot of fish working on yachts, so I've seen my fair share of seafood dishes, but halibut is easily one of my favorites. It's meaty, mild, and super versatile, which Makes it perfect for a simple but impressive meal like this. The Parmesan cheese crust adds a nice crunch on the outside while keeping the fish tender and flaky underneath. Paired with a quick lemon thyme sauce, it's fresh, flavorful, and doesn't need much else to shine.

1. Preheat the oven to 400°F (200°C).

2. Pat the halibut fillets dry with paper towels to ensure a good sear, then season both sides with salt and pepper.

3. Heat a large oven-safe skillet over medium-high heat and add 1 tablespoon of olive oil. When the oil is hot and shimmering, carefully lay the halibut fillets in the skillet.

4. Sear each side for 2 to 3 minutes until a golden crust forms. Remove the halibut and set aside; it will finish cooking from the residual heat. Brush the tops with a little olive oil to help the Parmesan panko topping stick.

5. In a small bowl, combine the Parmesan cheese, breadcrumbs, and parsley. Press this mixture onto the top of each halibut fillet, forming an even, crunchy crust.

6. Return the crusted fillets to the skillet and bake for 8 to 10 minutes, until the fish flakes easily with a fork and the crust is golden brown.

7. While the fish bakes, melt the butter in a medium saucepan over medium heat. Add the garlic and cook until it's fragrant, about 1 minute.

8. Pour in the white wine, allowing it to simmer and reduce by half, roughly 3 to 4 minutes.

9. Stir in the heavy cream, lemon zest, lemon juice, and thyme. Add a teaspoon of olive oil and season with salt and pepper. Simmer for 3 to 4 minutes, whisking gently until slightly thickened.

10. Remove the halibut from the oven, place each fillet on a plate, and spoon the creamy lemon thyme sauce over the top. Garnish with thyme or a sprinkle of lemon zest for an extra pop of flavor.

PAN-SEARED BEEF TENDERLOIN WITH TWO SIGNATURE SAUCES

SERVES 4

BEEF TENDERLOINS

4 6 oz. (170 g) beef tenderloin steaks, good quality, preferably Angus beef, at room temperature

2 tbsp. (30 ml) olive oil (or other high-smoke-point oil)

¼ cup (57 g) unsalted butter

2–3 fresh rosemary or thyme sprigs

3 garlic cloves, lightly smashed

Flaky sea salt and freshly ground black pepper to taste (for seasoning after cooking)

WHISKY MUSTARD SAUCE

2 tbsp. (28 g) unsalted butter

1 small shallot, finely minced

¼ cup (60 ml) whisky

½ cup (30 ml) heavy cream

1 tbsp. (15 g) Dijon mustard

2 tsp. (10 g) whole-grain mustard

Sea salt and freshly ground black pepper to taste

BLACK PEPPER ARMAGNAC SAUCE

2 tbsp. (28 g) unsalted butter

1 small shallot, finely minced

¼ cup (60 ml) Armagnac

½ cup (120 ml) heavy cream

2 tbsp. (10 g) lightly cracked black peppercorns

Sea salt to taste

"Steak for dinner. Powder for breakfast." That's the mountain way—fueling up with hearty indulgence before chasing fresh tracks at sunrise. One evening, after a lively dinner, some guests accidentally left behind a bottle of whisky. That moment became the spark for this dish, inspired by both the mountains and the whisky left behind. Take your beef tenderloin to new heights with a luxurious duo of sauces, each crafted to elevate its melt-in-your-mouth perfection. The first—a bold whisky and mustard blend—delivers smoky depth with a tangy kick, perfectly complementing the meat's richness. The second, a black pepper and Armagnac sauce, adds refined warmth and gentle heat, striking the perfect balance of elegance and spice. Together, they create an unforgettable contrast of flavors, making every bite as thrilling as the slopes themselves.

BEEF TENDERLOINS

1. Remove the beef tenderloin steaks from the refrigerator at least 30 minutes before cooking. This allows them to come to room temperature and ensures even cooking.

2. Preheat the oven to 400°F (200°C). Meanwhile, place a large oven-safe skillet (preferably cast iron) on the stove over medium-high heat.

3. Once the skillet is hot, add a drizzle of olive oil and heat until it just begins to smoke. Gently place the steaks in the pan, making sure they don't touch (this ensures a good sear). Sear the steaks for 2 to 3 minutes per side until a rich deep-brown crust forms. Avoid moving the steaks around during this process to ensure an even sear.

4. Once the steaks are seared, add the butter, rosemary or thyme, and garlic to the skillet. Tilt the pan slightly so the butter pools and use a spoon to baste the steaks with the melted herb-infused butter for about 1 minute. This step adds moisture and enhances the flavor.

5. Transfer the skillet to the oven. Roast the steaks for 5 to 8 minutes for medium-rare, or until the internal temperature reaches 125–130°F (52–54°C). For medium steaks, roast for an additional 2 to 3 minutes, aiming for an internal temperature of 135–140°F (57–60°C).

MAINS TO MELT THE SNOW

TIP: Use a meat thermometer for accuracy—this is the key to getting them just right!

6   Once the steaks are done, carefully remove the skillet from the oven and transfer the steaks to a cutting board. Tent them loosely with foil and let them rest for 5 to 10 minutes to allow the juices to redistribute. This step is essential for tender, juicy steaks.

7   Sprinkle each steak with a pinch of salt and a few twists of freshly ground black pepper to enhance the natural flavors. Serve with your choice of sides and drizzle with your signature sauces—whisky mustard and black pepper Armagnac—for a delicious finish.

WHISKY MUSTARD SAUCE

8 In a small saucepan, melt the butter over medium heat. Once melted, add the shallot and sauté for about 2 minutes until softened and translucent. Stir occasionally to prevent burning.

9 Carefully pour in the whisky and stir. Let it simmer and cook for about 3 to 4 minutes, until the liquid reduces by half and the alcohol evaporates, leaving behind a rich, concentrated flavor.

10 Stir in the heavy cream, whole grain and Dijon mustard, whisking until smooth. Continue to simmer for 2 to 3 minutes, allowing the sauce to thicken to your desired consistency.

11 Taste the sauce and season with salt and pepper to balance the flavors. Once thickened and seasoned, remove from the heat and serve immediately.

BLACK PEPPER ARMAGNAC SAUCE

12 In a separate saucepan, melt the butter over medium heat.

13 Once melted, add the shallot and cook, stirring occasionally, for about 2 to 3 minutes, or until softened and translucent. Add the peppercorns to the pan and cook, stirring frequently, for 1 to 2 minutes. This will allow the peppercorns to release their oils and soften, infusing the sauce with a deep, aromatic flavor.

14 Carefully pour in the Armagnac, stirring to combine with the shallots and peppercorns. Let the Armagnac cook for 3 to 4 minutes, simmering until reduced by half. This step will concentrate the flavors and mellow the peppercorns even further.

15 Stir in the heavy cream and continue to simmer the sauce for 3 to 4 minutes, allowing it to thicken slightly, stirring occasionally to ensure the sauce doesn't separate or burn. By now, the peppercorns should be soft and have imparted their flavors to the sauce.

16 Taste the sauce and season with salt to balance the flavors.

17 If the sauce is too thick, add a splash more cream or a little water to adjust the consistency.

18 Spoon the sauce over each tenderloin steak, making sure to include the softened peppercorns for texture. For a polished presentation, serve the sauce in individual bowls on the side, allowing guests to enjoy the unique flavor profile alongside your whisky mustard sauce.

SERVES

4

4 salmon fillets about 6 oz. (170 g) each

Pinch of sea salt and freshly ground black pepper

2 tbsp. (30 ml) olive oil, divided

12 large prawns (peeled and deveined)

3 garlic cloves (minced)

½ cup (60 g) sun-dried tomatoes (finely chopped, packed in oil)

1 tsp. finely chopped fresh oregano

½ cup (120 ml) white wine (or vegetable broth)

½ cup (120 ml) tomato passata

½ cup (120 ml) heavy cream

Sea salt and a grind of black pepper to taste

Fresh parsley (for garnish)

SALMON WITH PRAWNS IN A SUN-DRIED TOMATO AND OREGANO SAUCE

There's something undeniably tempting about perfectly seared salmon and juicy prawns nestled in a rich sun-dried tomato and oregano sauce. After spending time in Italy, I couldn't resist drawing on its bold, vibrant flavors. This dish channels the warmth of the Mediterranean—the earthy oregano and sweet sun-dried tomatoes bringing the Italian coast straight to the mountains. Including salmon, a Canadian staple, felt only natural, offering a familiar taste of home. Elegant yet comforting, this dish is made for a cozy night in, serving up sunshine no matter how snowy it is outside.

1. Pat the salmon fillets dry with paper towels—this helps to get that perfect sear! Season both sides with a pinch of salt and pepper.

2. Heat 1 tablespoon of olive oil in a large skillet over medium-high heat. Place the salmon skin-side down and cook for 3 to 4 minutes until golden. Flip gently, cook for 1 more minute, then remove and set aside—it will finish cooking in the sauce.

3. In the same skillet, add the remaining tablespoon of olive oil. Toss in the prawns, season with a little salt, and cook for 1 to 2 minutes per side until pink and golden. Remove the prawns from the skillet and set aside with the salmon.

4. Turn the heat to medium and add the garlic to the skillet. Let it sizzle for about 30 seconds until fragrant, but don't let it brown. Add the sun-dried tomatoes and oregano, stirring for 1 minute to release their flavors.

5. Pour in the white wine (or broth) and scrape up any browned bits from the bottom of the skillet. Let the wine reduce for 2 to 3 minutes.

6. Stir in the passata and simmer for 3 to 4 minutes. Add the heavy cream, combine, and simmer for 5 minutes until thickened. Season to taste with salt and pepper.

7. Return the salmon and prawns to the skillet. Spoon some of the sauce over each piece and let them warm through for 1 to 2 minutes.

8. Garnish with parsley. Plate each person with a salmon fillet, a few prawns, and a generous spoonful of the creamy sauce on top.

SEARED SCALLOPS WITH SALSA VERDE AGRODOLCE

SERVES

2-3

SALSA VERDE

1 cup (40 g) fresh parsley leaves

½ cup (20 g) fresh basil leaves

¼ cup (20 g) fresh mint leaves

2 tbsp. (20 g) capers, drained

1 garlic clove, minced

Zest and juice of 1 lemon

4 quality anchovy fillets

1 tbsp. (15 g) Dijon mustard

¼ cup (60 ml) olive oil

Sea salt and freshly ground black pepper to taste

SCALLOPS

12 large sea scallops, cleaned and patted dry

Sea salt and freshly ground black pepper to taste

1 tbsp. (15 ml) olive oil

1 tbsp. (14 g) unsalted butter

Who says lodge fare can't have a touch of elegance? These seared scallops with salsa Verde bring a refreshing twist to alpine dining, combining a golden-brown crust with a vibrant herb-packed sauce I've come to rely on time and time again. I use salsa Verde for so many things—it's one of those go-to staples that never fails to lift a dish—and I think it pairs especially well with scallops. The bright hit of fresh herbs and a touch of lemon balance the richness beautifully. It's a simple yet indulgent dish, perfect as a light main or a refined appetizer to keep the mountain spirit going.

SALSA VERDE

1. Gather the parsley, basil, and mint on a large cutting board. Chop them finely until they're well-blended and look like forest-green confetti.

2. Sprinkle the capers over the herbs and give everything a few more chops so the capers start to mingle with the greens.

3. Sprinkle the garlic, lemon zest, and anchovy fillets onto the herb mixture. Chop everything together until the anchovies and garlic are finely integrated, creating a fragrant, vibrant green mixture that smells fresh and delicious.

4. Transfer the chopped mixture to a bowl, then add the lemon juice and Dijon mustard. Stir until smooth—the mustard will add a subtle tang that brings all the flavors together.

5. Slowly drizzle in the ¼ cup olive oil as you stir, watching the salsa Verde turn into a smooth, lush sauce. Taste and season with a pinch of sea salt and a few twists of black pepper to balance everything perfectly. Set the sauce aside while you prepare the scallops

SCALLOPS

6. Heat 1 tablespoon olive oil in a large skillet over medium-high heat. You'll know the oil is ready when it begins to shimmer.

7. Carefully add the scallops to the pan, ensuring they aren't crowded so they can sear evenly. Let them cook undisturbed for 2 to 3 minutes on each side, until they form a golden-brown crust while remaining tender inside.

MAINS TO MELT THE SNOW

8   In the last minute of cooking, add the butter to the pan. Use a spoon to baste the scallops with the melted butter, giving them a rich, finishing touch without overcooking.

9   Spoon a bit of salsa Verde onto each plate as a base, then nestle three scallops on top. Drizzle a little more salsa Verde over everything if desired for an extra burst of color and flavor. Serve immediately.

MAPLE-BALSAMIC PORK TENDERLOIN WITH CREAMY LEEKS

SERVES

4

PORK TENDERLOIN

2 pork tenderloins (about 1 lb. each)

2 tbsp. (30 ml) olive oil

1 + ½ tsp. salt

Freshly ground black pepper to taste

MAPLE BALSAMIC SAUCE

1 tbsp. (15 ml) olive oil

2 garlic cloves, minced

¼ cup (60 ml) balsamic vinegar

¼ cup (60 ml) pure maple syrup

1 tbsp. (15 g) Dijon mustard

1 tsp. (1 g) finely chopped fresh thyme leaves

LEEKS

2 tbsp. (28 g) unsalted butter

3 large leeks, white and light green parts only, sliced thinly

½ cup (120 ml) heavy cream

Sea salt and freshly ground black pepper to taste

1 tsp. (1 g) lemon zest (optional, for brightness)

This dish brings together the rich flavors of roasted pork with a sweet and tangy maple balsamic sauce served on the side. The pork is oven-roasted to tender perfection, letting its natural richness shine, while the sauce adds a vibrant touch—ideal for dipping or drizzling, depending on your mood. It's paired with a side of creamy leeks, inspired by my time in London. We do love our leeks in the UK, and this soft, buttery version brings a familiar comfort and gentle elegance to the plate.

1. Preheat the oven to 400°F (200°C). Rub the pork tenderloins with the olive oil, salt, and pepper.

2. In a large ovenproof skillet, heat the olive oil over medium-high heat. Sear the pork on all sides until browned, about 3 to 4 minutes per side.

3. Transfer the skillet to the oven and roast the pork for 20 to 25 minutes, or until a thermometer inserted into the center reads 145°F (63°C). Remove from the oven and let the pork rest.

4. In a small saucepan, warm up the olive oil over medium heat. Toss in the garlic, letting it sizzle and fill the kitchen with that mouthwatering aroma—about 1 to 2 minutes should do the trick.

5. Next, pour in the balsamic vinegar, maple syrup, Dijon mustard, and thyme, stirring them together. Now bring the sauce to a gentle simmer, stirring now and then as it reduces into a glossy, slightly thickened perfection—about 5 to 7 minutes. Season with a pinch of salt and pepper, then set it aside to cool and thicken just a bit more.

6. While your pork is roasting away, melt the butter in a large skillet over medium heat, letting it sizzle and get all bubbly. Toss in the leeks with a pinch of salt and stir them around. Let them cook for about 10 minutes until tender. Now, pour in the heavy cream, giving it a good stir, and let it simmer for another 2 to 3 minutes until the cream thickens up and coats the leeks. Season with salt, pepper, and if you're feeling fancy, a bit of lemon zest for that bright pop of flavor.

7. Arrange the creamy leeks on a serving platter as a bed for the pork. Slice the pork loin and place the slices on top of the leeks. Drizzle the maple balsamic sauce over the pork and serve any extra sauce on the side for additional drizzling.

DUCK BREAST WITH SWEET ORANGE AND CRANBERRY SAUCE

SERVES

4

DUCK BREAST

4 duck breasts (with skin on)

1 tbsp. (15 g) coarse sea salt

1 tbsp. (3 g) roughly chopped fresh thyme leaves

Freshly ground black pepper

ORANGE AND CRANBERRY SAUCE

1 tbsp. (15 ml) olive oil

1 small shallot, finely chopped

1 garlic clove, minced

½ cup (120 ml) freshly squeezed orange juice (about 1 large orange)

¼ cup (60 ml) chicken stock

¼ cup (60 g) cranberry sauce (or fresh cranberries if preferred)

1 tbsp. (15 ml) maple syrup or honey

1 tbsp. (14 g) unsalted butter (optional, for richness)

Sea salt and freshly ground black pepper to taste

This crispy-seared duck breast brings back memories of a certain London restaurant where we used to cook a lot of duck, always aiming for that perfect balance of richness and refinement. This version is my alpine take on it—juicy, tender, and cooked to perfection, topped with a bold orange and cranberry sauce that's bright, tangy, and just sweet enough. It's the kind of dish that feels like a celebration without being fussy. This dish always gets applause—and usually a request for seconds.

1. Score the skin of the duck breasts in a crisscross pattern with a sharp knife (this helps the fat render, and the skin get crispy). Be sure not to cut into the meat itself! Rub the salt and thyme into the scored skin, making sure every inch is coated. Season the flesh side with pepper for a little extra zing. Let the duck breasts sit at room temperature for 10 to 15 minutes.

2. Heat a large ovenproof skillet over medium-high heat—no oil needed, the duck fat will do the work. Place the duck breasts skin-side down and sear for 6 to 7 minutes until golden and crispy, draining excess fat if needed. Flip and cook 3 to 4 minutes more, until the internal temperature reaches 135°F (57°C) for medium-rare or 150°F (66°C) for well-done. Remove and let rest 5 to 10 minutes before making the sauce.

3. In the same skillet (with some of that glorious duck fat left behind), add the olive oil and sauté the shallot and garlic over medium heat for 2 to 3 minutes until they're soft and aromatic. Pour in the orange juice and chicken stock, giving everything a good stir. Scrape up any tasty bits from the bottom of the pan—you want all that flavor! Add the cranberry sauce (or cranberries) and maple syrup or honey. Stir it all together and let it simmer for 5 to 7 minutes, allowing the sauce to reduce and thicken up nicely. Taste and adjust the seasoning with salt and pepper. For that final touch, stir in a tablespoon of butter for a rich, glossy finish.

4. Slice the rested duck breasts against the grain and arrange them on plates. Spoon the orange and cranberry sauce over the duck or serve it on the side for dipping.

CRISPY LEMON BASIL CHICKEN WITH ROASTED RED PEPPER SAUCE

SERVES

4

LEMON BASIL MARINADE

Zest and juice of 2 lemons

2 tbsp. (5 g) finely chopped fresh basil

2 garlic cloves, minced

2 tbsp. (30 ml) olive oil

1 tsp. (7 g) honey

½ tsp. (1 g) finely chopped fresh oregano

Sea salt and freshly ground black pepper to taste

4 boneless, skinless chicken breasts

ROASTED RED PEPPER SAUCE

2 red bell peppers, roasted and peeled

1 tbsp. (15 ml) olive oil

1 small shallot, finely chopped

2 garlic cloves, minced

½ cup (120 ml) chicken or vegetable stock

1 tsp. (5 g) balsamic vinegar

Sea salt and freshly ground black pepper to taste

1 tsp. (finely chopped fresh basil

1 tbsp. (15 ml) heavy cream (optional, for richness)

This dish is all about bright, fresh flavors that come together in a simple yet stunning way. Inspired by my years of cooking in the Mediterranean, it draws especially from southern Italy, where peppers are everywhere when you're provisioning—bright, bold, and sturdy enough to find their way into just about everything. I've always loved their versatility, and here, they shine in a rich, smoky roasted red pepper sauce that adds depth to the lemon and basil chicken. The chicken itself is pan-fried to perfection—crisp on the outside, juicy and tender on the inside—offering the kind of light but comforting winter fare that still feels indulgent. It brings a little Mediterranean sunshine to your mountain table.

1. In a bowl, combine the zest and juice of those lemons (bring on the citrus!), basil, garlic, olive oil, honey, oregano, salt, and pepper. Whisk it all together until well mixed.

2. Add the chicken breasts and give them a good toss, making sure they're all coated in that lemony, basil goodness. Cover and pop them in the fridge for at least 30 minutes, or up to 2 hours to let those flavors infuse.

3. If using fresh red peppers, place them on a baking sheet and roast under the broiler, flipping occasionally until the skin's all charred and blistered (about 10 minutes). Then, throw them in a bowl, cover it up, and let them steam for 10 minutes. Peel off the skin, scoop out the seeds, and chop up the flesh like a pro.

4. In a saucepan, heat the olive oil over medium heat. Add the shallot and sauté for about 2 to 3 minutes until it's all soft and fragrant (smell that goodness?).

5. Add the garlic and cook for another minute, letting it mingle with the shallots.

6. Toss in the red pepper, chicken or vegetable stock, and balsamic vinegar, stirring it all together. Let it simmer for 5 to 7 minutes, letting those flavors get to know each other.

7. Blend the sauce until smooth using an immersion blender or regular blender. If you're feeling fancy, stir in a little heavy cream for a rich, velvety finish. Taste, then season with salt, pepper, and basil.

8. Heat a skillet over medium-high heat and add a tablespoon of olive oil. Now, don't be shy—get that pan nice and hot!

9. Take the chicken out of the marinade and sear it in the pan for 5 to 7 minutes per side, or until the skin's golden brown and crispy and the internal temperature hits 165°F (75°C). Don't overcrowd the pan; cook in batches if needed. You want crispy, not soggy.

10. Heat a large skillet over medium-high heat. Add a tablespoon of olive oil.

11. Remove the chicken from the marinade and cook it in the hot skillet for 5 to 7 minutes per side, or until golden brown and cooked through (internal temperature should reach 165°F [75°C]). Be careful not to overcrowd the pan—cook in batches if necessary.

12. Once the chicken is cooked, let it rest for a few minutes—this gives the juices time to settle, so each bite is as tender and flavorful as possible! Slice the chicken and arrange it on plates. Serve the smoky, sweet roasted red pepper sauce on the side for drizzling or dipping.

MOUNTAIN LODGE CHICKEN WITH RED WINE MUSHROOM SAUCE

SERVES

4

- 4 boneless, skinless chicken breasts
- Sea salt and freshly ground black pepper to taste
- 2 tbsp. (30 ml) olive oil, divided
- 1 tbsp. (14 g) unsalted butter
- 1 medium onion, finely chopped
- 2 garlic cloves, minced
- 2 cups (about 250 g) mushrooms, sliced (cremini or button mushrooms work best for that woodsy flavor)
- 1 cup (240 ml) dry red wine (something bold and fruity if you're feeling fancy)
- 1 tsp. (5 g) sugar
- 2 tsp. (10 g) freshly squeezed lemon juice
- 1 cup (240 ml) chicken broth
- 1 tbsp. (3 g) finely chopped fresh thyme leaves
- 1 tbsp. (3 g) chopped fresh parsley (for garnish)

Sometimes, a simple chicken breast just needs a little extra oomph—and this rich red wine and mushroom sauce delivers in spades. It's my pared-back nod to the classic coq au vin, with all those deep, soulful flavors packed into a quicker, simpler dish. The chicken is seared to golden perfection, then bathed in a velvety sauce loaded with earthy mushrooms and bold red wine. It's rustic, robust, and full of character. Comforting yet elevated, it's the kind of dish that feels like a warm hug with a glass of something good on the side.

1. Pat the chicken breasts dry, then season both sides generously with salt and pepper.

2. Heat 1 tablespoon olive oil in a sturdy large skillet over medium-high heat. Add the chicken breasts and sear for 4 to 5 minutes per side, until golden brown and cooked through (internal temperature should reach 165°F [74°C]). Once done, transfer the chicken to a plate, cover with foil, and set aside to rest.

3. In the same skillet, add the remaining olive oil and butter. Add the onion, stirring for 4 to 5 minutes until it softens and becomes aromatic. Toss in the garlic and mushrooms, cooking until the mushrooms turn golden and caramelized, about 5 to 7 minutes.

4. Here's the fun part! Pour in that bold red wine, scraping up any flavorful browned bits from the skillet's bottom—this adds tons of depth to the sauce. Stir in the sugar for a gentle sweetness, then squeeze in the lemon juice for a fresh kick. Let the wine simmer and reduce by half, about 5 minutes.

5. Pour in the chicken broth and sprinkle in the thyme, letting everything simmer together for another 5 minutes to develop a rich, hearty flavor.

6. Arrange each chicken breast on a plate, then spoon a generous helping of the zesty mushroom sauce over the top. Sprinkle with fresh parsley for a pop of color and extra freshness.

ON THE SIDE

These sides are here to complete your meal—mix and match them or let each one shine on its own. They might not take center stage, but they're more than ready to steal a little of the spotlight when it counts. This chapter brings balance to the mains that melt the snow.

ALPINE PARMESAN RISOTTO

SERVES
4

5 cups (1.2 L) chicken or vegetable broth, kept warm

2 tbsp. (30 ml) olive oil

3 tbsp. (43 g) unsalted butter, divided

1 medium onion, finely chopped

2 garlic cloves, minced

1 ½ cups (300 g) Arborio rice

½ cup (120 ml) dry white wine

1 cup (100 g) freshly grated Parmesan cheese, extra for sprinkling

Sea salt to taste

Grind of black pepper

Chopped fresh parsley or chives (for garnish)

When the mountain air turns crisp and the slopes call it a day, nothing brings that cozy lodge feeling quite like a bowl of creamy Parmesan risotto. I've made this dish countless times over the years—whether tucked into a tiny galley kitchen off the coast of Sicily or in a luxurious chalet in the Alps—and it never fails to warm both hearts and bellies. It's simple, but luxurious: nutty Parmesan cheese folded into silky, perfectly cooked rice, each spoonful a little taste of indulgence after a day of snow and adventure.

1. Start by keeping the broth warm in a saucepan over low heat. Risotto loves warm broth—it helps the rice cook smoothly and stay creamy.

2. In a large heavy-bottomed pan, heat the olive oil and 2 tablespoons of butter over medium heat. Add the onion and cook, stirring occasionally, until it's soft and translucent, about 5 minutes. Add the garlic and cook for another minute until fragrant.

3. Stir in the Arborio rice, letting it toast lightly in the oil and butter for 1 to 2 minutes. The rice should start to look slightly translucent around the edges—this helps it absorb the flavors right from the start.

4. Pour the wine in now and stir continuously until it is mostly absorbed. This adds an extra layer of flavor to the risotto.

5. Add one ladle of warm broth to the rice, stirring constantly. Keep stirring until nearly all the liquid is absorbed—this part is key. Once the rice has soaked up the broth, add another ladle and continue stirring. Repeat this process, adding one ladle at a time and letting it absorb fully each time, for about 18 to 20 minutes. You'll notice the rice becoming creamy and tender with a slight bite at the center.

6. Once the rice is perfectly creamy, remove the pan from the heat. Stir in the remaining tablespoon of butter and Parmesan cheese, mixing until the risotto is smooth and velvety. Season with salt and pepper to taste.

7. Spoon the risotto into four bowls, sprinkle with a little extra Parmesan cheese, and garnish with parsley or chives for a touch of color. Serve immediately.

SERVES

4

3 strips thick-cut bacon, diced

1 lb. (450 g) brussels sprouts, trimmed and halved

2 tbsp. (30 ml) olive oil

Sea salt and freshly ground black pepper to taste

2 tbsp. (30 ml) pure maple syrup

2 tbsp. (20 g) toasted almonds (optional, for crunch)

MAPLE-GLAZED BRUSSELS SPROUTS WITH CRISPY BACON

Who knew brussels sprouts could be so irresistible? This dish was born out of one of those "use what you've got" moments—I had a bag of sprouts, a few strips of bacon, and a bottle of maple syrup, and needed to whip something up fast. The result? A total game changer. Roasted until golden and crispy, the sprouts get a glossy drizzle of maple and a scatter of smoky, crunchy bacon bits—simple ingredients that come together in the most delicious way. Sweet, salty, and downright addictive, this side has since become a firm favorite for lodge dinners and cozy gatherings.

1. Preheat the oven to 400°F (200°C). Grab a large baking sheet and set it aside.

2. Spread the bacon on the baking sheet and pop it in the oven for about 8 minutes, just until it starts to crisp up and release all that delicious bacon fat.

3. While the bacon's cooking, toss the brussels sprouts in a large bowl with the olive oil, a good pinch of salt, and a few cracks of pepper.

4. Take the sheet out of the oven and add the brussels sprouts right on top of the bacon. Give them a gentle toss to coat everything in the bacon fat and spread them out in a single layer. Roast for 20 to 25 minutes, stirring halfway, until the brussels sprouts are golden and crispy.

5. Drizzle the maple syrup over the brussels sprouts and bacon and roast for another 5 minutes. This lets the syrup caramelize a bit, adding a warm sweetness.

6. Sprinkle the almonds or pecans on top if using and serve warm. These sprouts are best enjoyed right out of the oven when they're at their crispiest!

ON THE SIDE

GARLIC PARMESAN ROASTED BROCCOLI

SERVES
4

1 large head of broccoli, cut into florets

2 tbsp. (30 ml) olive oil

3 garlic cloves, minced

Zest of 1 lemon

Sea salt and freshly ground black pepper to taste

¼ cup (25 g) grated Parmesan cheese

3 tbsp. (45 ml) freshly squeezed lemon juice

Say goodbye to bland broccoli! This recipe was born one winter season when I decided to transform the humble green floret into something people couldn't wait to eat. With crispy, golden edges, a rich garlic punch, and a cheesy finish, this dish makes you forget it's even a vegetable! Roasting brings out the broccoli's natural sweetness, and the combination of Parmesan cheese and garlic elevates it to a whole new level of flavor. This side dish is proof that healthy can absolutely steal the show.

1. Preheat the oven to 425°F (220°C). Line a baking sheet with parchment paper.

2. In a large bowl, toss the broccoli florets with the olive oil, garlic, lemon zest, salt, and pepper. The lemon zest will add a fresh citrusy zing to the dish, balancing the flavors.

3. Spread the broccoli evenly on the prepared baking sheet. Roast for 15 to 20 minutes, flipping halfway through, until the broccoli is golden and crispy on the edges.

4. In the last 5 minutes of roasting, sprinkle the Parmesan cheese over the broccoli to melt and create a delicious cheesy crust.

5. Remove from the oven, squeeze a little lemon juice over the top (if desired), and serve immediately.

CRISP WINTER COLESLAW

SERVES
4

2 cups (150 g) very finely shredded green cabbage

1 cup (75 g) very finely shredded red cabbage

2 medium carrots, grated

2 scallions, thinly sliced

¼ cup (60 g) mayonnaise

¼ cup (60 g) sour cream

1 tbsp. (15 ml) apple cider vinegar (for a little zip!)

1 tsp. (5 g) Dijon mustard (the secret ingredient)

1 tsp. (7 g) honey

Sea salt and freshly ground black pepper to taste

1 tbsp. (1 g) chopped cilantro (for a final flourish)

Who says winter meals need to be all about rich, heavy flavors? After years of grilling up delicious barbecues, I've learned that a good slaw can bring the perfect balance to any meal. This side dish is a nod to those classic barbecue days, with its vibrant mix of shredded cabbage, fresh scallions, and a tangy-creamy dressing. It's a dish that pairs perfectly with hearty winter meals, offering a light and refreshing contrast that keeps things exciting.

1. In a large bowl, combine the green cabbage, red cabbage, carrot, and scallions. Shredding the cabbage very fine is key to achieving a light, even texture in every bite. The cabbage also absorbs the dressing better, resulting in a more flavorful slaw.

2. In a small bowl, mix the mayo, sour cream, apple cider vinegar, Dijon mustard, and honey. Don't forget a pinch of salt and pepper!

3. Pour the dressing over the shredded veggie mix. Give it a good toss until everything is luxuriously coated and ready to shine.

4. If you prefer cold coleslaw, cover your slaw and let it chill in the fridge for about 30 minutes. This gives it time to soak up all the flavors and become even more delicious.

5. Give it one last toss, sprinkle with cilantro, and dive in.

DEEP-STUFFED POTATOES

SERVES

4

4 large russet potatoes

2 tbsp. (30 ml) olive oil

½ cup finely chopped kielbasa

1 onion, finely diced

½ cup (120 g) sour cream

¼ cup (60 ml) milk

¼ cup (57 g) unsalted butter, melted

Sea salt and freshly ground black pepper to taste

1 cup (113 g) Monterey Jack or pepper jack cheese, divided

¼ cup chopped chives, divided

These deep-stuffed potatoes are twice-baked bundles of comfort that speak straight to my Polish roots—where potatoes are practically a love language. Their crispy, golden shells cradle a rich, melty filling of sharp cheese, chives, and smoky kielbasa, with a dollop of sour cream for that familiar, tangy finish. It's everything I love about cozy, home-style cooking: hearty, nostalgic, and a little bit indulgent.

1. Preheat the oven to 400°F (200°C). Scrub the potatoes clean, then rub each one with olive oil and sprinkle generously with salt. Place the potatoes directly on the oven rack and bake for 50 to 60 minutes, or until tender and easily pierced with a fork. Remove from the oven and let cool slightly.

2. While the potatoes are baking, heat a skillet over medium heat and cook the kielbasa until golden and crisp around the edges, about 5 to 7 minutes. Remove and set aside. In the same skillet—using the rendered fat or adding 1 tablespoon of butter or oil—add the onions. Cook over medium-low heat, stirring often, until soft, golden, and caramelized, about 10 to 15 minutes.

3. Once the potatoes are cool enough to handle, slice them in half lengthwise. Scoop out the flesh into a mixing bowl, leaving a thin layer of potato to support the skins. Mash the potato with sour cream, milk, and melted butter until smooth and creamy. Season with salt and pepper to taste. Fold in half of the cheddar cheese, the kielbasa, the caramelized onions, and half the chives.

4. Spoon the mashed filling back into the potato shells, mounding it slightly. Arrange the stuffed potatoes on a baking sheet.

5. Reduce the oven temperature to 375°F (190°C). Top each potato with the remaining cheddar cheese. Return to the oven and bake for 15 to 20 minutes, or until the cheese is melted, bubbly, and lightly golden on top.

6. Sprinkle with the remaining chives before serving for a fresh finish.

SERVES

4

4 medium sweet potatoes, peeled and cut into 1-inch cubes

3 tbsp. (45 ml) coconut oil, melted

Sea salt and freshly ground black pepper to taste

Dash of cinnamon (optional)

1 tbsp. (2 g) lime zest (freshly grated for that pop of zing)

¼ cup (25 g) freshly grated Parmesan cheese

"OLD YANKEE" ROASTED SWEET POTATOES

These roasted sweet potatoes, glazed with rich coconut oil, are a beloved favorite of the "Old Yankees"—a group of American skiers who have been skiing in the region for many years. They first met Colleen at her outdoor shop, Wearabouts, back when K3 was still a fun project. Since then, they've returned every year, now bringing their sons to carry on the tradition. Like these sweet, caramelized potatoes, their visits bring warmth and sunshine to every gathering.

1. Preheat the oven to 400°F (200°C). Line a baking sheet with parchment paper, because who wants extra cleanup?

2. In a big bowl, give the sweet potatoes a loving toss with the melted coconut oil, salt, pepper, and a dash of cinnamon (if you're feeling fancy). Make sure each cube gets a nice coat!

3. Spread the sweet potatoes out on the baking sheet in a single layer. Pop them into the oven and let them roast for about 25 to 30 minutes, flipping halfway through. You're looking for crispy edges and tender insides—trust us, it's worth the wait!

4. Once they're golden and gorgeous, take the sweet potatoes out of the oven and immediately grate lime zest over the top. Then, sprinkle on that Parmesan cheese like its confetti—let it melt into the warm potatoes.

5. Gently toss to combine all the flavors, and voilà! You've got a side dish that's sure to wow.

CRISPY SMASHED POTATOES

SERVES
4–6

1 ½ lb. (680 g) baby or small Yukon Gold potatoes (or any waxy variety)

2 tbsp. (30 ml) olive oil

3 tbsp. (43 g) unsalted butter, melted

Sea salt and freshly ground black pepper to taste

Fresh herbs like rosemary, thyme, or parsley (for garnish)

The best of both worlds—crispy on the outside, fluffy on the inside! These smashed potatoes became a bit of a go-to during one especially snowy winter season when I needed something comforting, quick, and just plain fun to make. A gentle smash, a generous glug of olive oil, and into a hot oven they go—until those golden edges turn irresistibly crisp and the centers stay beautifully soft and pillowy. They're simple, sure, but absolutely packed with personality and flavor.

1. Place the potatoes in a large pot and cover with water. Add a generous pinch of salt and bring to a boil. Lower the heat to a simmer and cook the potatoes for 15 to 20 minutes, or until they are fork-tender but not falling apart. Drain the potatoes and let them cool for a few minutes.

2. Preheat the oven to 425°F (220°C). Line a baking sheet with parchment paper. Place the boiled potatoes on the baking sheet, spaced apart. Use a fork or the bottom of a glass to gently smash each potato until they are about ½-inch thick. Don't smash too hard—you want them to stay together but get crispy on the edges.

3. In a small bowl, combine the olive oil and melted butter. Drizzle this mixture over the smashed potatoes, making sure each one is generously coated. Season with salt and pepper. Roast in the oven for 20 to 25 minutes, or until the edges are golden brown and crispy. Remove from the oven, brush some more melted butter on each potato, season, and return to the oven for about 7 to 8 minutes.

4. Once the potatoes are crispy and golden, remove them from the oven. Garnish with herbs like rosemary or parsley and serve hot. For an extra treat, serve with a dollop of sour cream or a squeeze of lemon on the side.

SILKY CAULIFLOWER PUREE

SERVES

4

¼ cup (57 g) unsalted butter (because butter is the secret to magic)

1 yellow onion, chopped

2 garlic cloves, minced

1 fresh thyme sprig

2 medium heads of cauliflower (about 1 ½ lb. [680 g] each), chopped into florets

1 cup (240 ml) vegetable broth (or chicken broth, if you're feeling fancy)

¾ cup (180 ml) heavy cream

1 tbsp. (15 ml) olive oil

A squeeze of lemon juice (to brighten up the flavors)

Sea salt and freshly ground black pepper to taste (don't be shy with the seasoning)

Fresh chives or parsley (for garnish) (optional, but adds that finishing touch)

Who knew cauliflower could be so luxurious? This silky-smooth puree came to life after a few lodge guests asked for something a little lighter than the usual potatoes—something comforting, but not quite so heavy. The result? A velvety, elegant side dish that still delivers on richness, without weighing you down!

1. Heat a large pot over medium heat and melt the butter. Add the onion and garlic to the pot and sauté for 8 to 10 minutes, until they're soft and aromatic. This is where the flavor base is built, so give it time to turn into a fragrant, savory foundation.

2. Toss in the thyme and cauliflower florets. Stir everything together so that the cauliflower gets some love from the butter, garlic, and onion. Now, it's time for the liquids: Pour in the vegetable broth and heavy cream, just enough to cover the cauliflower. Bring it to a boil, then reduce the heat to a simmer. Let the cauliflower cook for 20 to 25 minutes, or until it's meltingly tender. Here's the trick: Pay attention to the liquid level! You're making a puree, not a soup, so keep the liquids just enough to soften the cauliflower without making it too runny. If you need to, you can add a little more broth or cream if it gets too thick.

3. Once the cauliflower is soft and cooked through, remove the thyme sprig and discard it. Scoop everything—the cauliflower, onion, and garlic—into a blender or food processor. Add the olive oil and lemon juice to bring everything together. If the mixture feels a bit thick, you can add a little more broth or cream until it reaches that perfect velvety texture. The olive oil adds richness, while the lemon juice gives it that bright, zesty finish.

4. Taste your puree and adjust the seasoning with more salt and pepper if needed. Spoon it into four bowls, garnish with chives or parsley for a pop of color and serve hot.

BLUSHING OLIVE OIL MASHED POTATOES

SERVES

4

1 ½ lb. (680 g) Yukon Gold potatoes, peeled and cut into chunks

½ lb. (225 g) sweet potatoes, peeled and cut into chunks

2 tbsp. (28 g) unsalted butter

¼ cup (60 ml) heavy cream, warmed

¼ cup (60 ml) extra-virgin olive oil, more for drizzling

Sea salt and freshly ground black pepper to taste

Chopped fresh herbs such as chives, parsley, or thyme (for garnish, optional)

I've always loved adding sweet potato to regular mash—not just for the subtle sweetness, but for that gorgeous warm blush it brings to the plate. This vibrant mash blends creamy white potatoes with naturally sweet golden-orange sweet potatoes, all whipped together with a good drizzle of olive oil for a light, buttery finish. The result is velvety, rich, and full of earthy flavor—comforting yet bright, and just the thing to warm up a winter meal.

1. Place the Yukon Gold and sweet potatoes in a large pot. Cover with cold water, add a pinch of salt, and bring to a boil. Once boiling, reduce the heat to a simmer and cook for about 15 to 20 minutes, or until fork-tender.

2. Drain the potatoes well, then return them to the pot. For an ultra-smooth texture, pass the potatoes through a potato ricer into the pot. If you don't have a ricer, you can mash them with a regular potato masher.

3. Add the butter, olive oil, and warmed cream to the potatoes. Stir until smooth and creamy.

4. Season with salt and pepper to taste.

5. Spoon into four bowls, drizzle with extra olive oil, and garnish with herbs if desired.

ON THE SIDE

DESSERTS TO END YOUR DAY

After a day carving turns and chasing powder, the perfect ending is a little something sweet. This chapter is packed with desserts that warm the soul and satisfy every craving—from gooey, indulgent treats to rustic, comforting classics. Because at the lodge, dessert isn't just a finale; it's a celebration. Sweeten your après-ski with these crowd-pleasers!

SERVES
10

1 cup (227 g) unsalted butter, at room temperature

1 cup (200 g) sugar

½ cup (50 g) cocoa powder, sifted

1 tbsp. (15 ml) vanilla

4 eggs

½ cup (60 g) all-purpose flour

¼ tsp. (1.2 g) salt

1 + ½ cups (225 g) dark chocolate, chunks (70% cocoa)

¾ cup (100 g) white chocolate, chunks

½ cup (50 g) whole pecans

"DARK SIDE" CHOCOLATE BROWNIES

Like the legendary Dark Side run at K3—the part of the tenure where the snow is perfect, the runs are epic, and the skiing never disappoints—these brownies are an adventure in every bite. Deep, dark, and dangerously delicious, this is a recipe for the ultimate après-ski indulgence. And yes, I'll admit it—I stole this recipe from Andi, one of the talented chefs at K3, because who can resist a secret this sweet?

1. Preheat the oven to 350°F (175°C). Grab a 9 x 12-inch (23 x 30 cm) baking pan, and line it with parchment paper, your brownies' ticket to easy slicing. No parchment paper? Just grease it with butter until every corner shines.

2. In a microwave-safe bowl, melt the butter until it's silky and golden. Let it cool a bit; we want a smooth batter, not chocolate scrambled eggs! Then stir in the sugar and cocoa powder, watching it transform into a thick, velvety chocolate paste.

3. Add the vanilla.

4. Add the eggs, one at a time, beating well after each addition. This is your arm workout for the day. Keep mixing until the batter is smooth and glossy.

5. Sift together the flour and salt, and gradually add this to your chocolate mixture, stirring until just combined. Don't overmix. Brownies like to be handled gently.

6. Fold in those chocolate chunks and pecans, letting them nestle into the batter. Pour the mixture into your prepared pan, smoothing it to the edges for an even bake.

7. Bake for about 25 to 30 minutes, or until a toothpick inserted into the center comes out with just a few moist crumbs. Don't be deceived by the top—it will look not fully cooked, but once the brownies cool, you'll get that perfect fudgy texture. Remember, slightly underbaked brownies are the key to a rich, gooey bite!

8. Let the brownies cool in the pan for about 10 minutes before lifting them out using the parchment paper. Cool completely on a wire rack before slicing into squares.

9. Serve with a dollop of cream or a scoop of vanilla ice cream.

SERVES

10 OR 12

CRUST

2 cups (200 g) digestive biscuits (or Graham crackers if you're in the U.S.)

¼ cup (50 g) sugar

½ cup (113 g) unsalted butter, melted

¼ tsp. (1.5 g) salt

FILLING

4 (8-oz.) packages (900 g) cream cheese, at room temperature

1 cup (200 g) sugar

1 tsp. (5 g) vanilla

3 eggs

½ cup (120 g) sour cream

½ cup (120 ml) heavy cream

¼ cup (60 ml) freshly squeezed lemon juice

Zest of 3 or 4 lemons

STRAWBERRY COINTREAU COMPOTE

1 ½ cups (250 g) fresh strawberries (hulled)

¼ cup (30 g) powdered sugar

2 tbsp. (30 g) Cointreau (or your favorite orange liqueur)

1 tbsp. (2 g) fresh mint leaves (plus extra for garnish)

BAKED LEMON CHEESECAKE WITH STRAWBERRY COINTREAU COMPOTE

Skiing burns calories, right? So why not reward yourself with a dessert that's as bright and sunny as a Mallorca winter's day? This baked lemon cheesecake is my way of bringing a little island sunshine to snowy slopes. In Mallorca, lemons are so abundant that people leave baskets of them outside their houses for anyone to take—so naturally, I always have a stash ready for something zesty and delicious. This baked lemon cheesecake is a snow-capped masterpiece with a creamy, tangy filling that melts in your mouth. The real showstopper, though, is the fresh strawberry and Cointreau compote—a bright, boozy burst of sunshine that cuts through the richness like a well-timed ski turn.

1. Preheat the oven to 325°F (165°C). Grab a 9-inch (23 cm) springform pan and line the outside with heavy-duty aluminum foil. You'll want to make sure it's sealed tight so no water gets into the crust.

2. In a bowl, mix the digestive biscuit crumbs, sugar, melted butter and salt. Stir until everything is nicely combined and the crumbs are evenly coated in buttery goodness. Press the mixture into the bottom of your springform pan, creating a snug little base. Bake it at 325°F (165°C) for 10 to 12 minutes or until golden brown. Let it cool while prepping the creamy filling.

3. Beat the cream cheese until smooth and fluffy (no lumps allowed!). Add in the sugar and beat until it's all silky and sweet. Next, beat in the eggs, one at a time. Then add the sour cream, heavy cream, lemon juice, and lemon zest. Mix until everything is perfectly combined into a luscious, creamy batter.

4. Here's the secret to that crack-free, perfectly creamy cheesecake: the water bath. You're going to place your springform pan with the cheesecake batter into a large roasting pan or deep baking dish.

5. Carefully pour hot water into the roasting pan until it comes about halfway up the sides of the pan. This will help bake the cheesecake evenly, keeping it smooth and creamy. Make sure the water doesn't splash into the cheesecake batter.

6. Carefully slide your cheesecake (with the water bath) into the oven. Bake for 55 to 65 minutes at 325°F (165°C) until the edges are set but the center has a gentle wobble (think of it as a little jiggle, not a dance!). Don't worry if the top gets a little golden—this cheesecake likes to sunbathe. If you notice it's getting too golden, just loosely cover it with some foil during the last 20 minutes.

7. Once done, turn off the oven and leave the cheesecake in there with the door slightly ajar for 1 hour. This helps cool it slowly and prevents cracking. Grab a cup of cocoa and relax for a bit. After an hour, carefully remove the cheesecake from the oven and take it out of the water bath. Let it cool on a wire rack at room temperature.

8. For the smoothest, creamiest cheesecake, pop it in the fridge for at least 4 hours, or preferably overnight. This gives the cheesecake plenty of time to set up and become perfectly chilled.

9. In a blender, combine the strawberries, powdered sugar, Cointreau, and mint leaves. Blend until smooth, adjusting the sweetness or Cointreau if necessary.

10. Once chilled, run a knife around the edge of the cheesecake to loosen it from the pan. Then, remove the springform pan's sides and marvel at that gorgeous, crack-free cheesecake you just created. Drizzle the strawberry and Cointreau sauce over the top of the cheesecake. Garnish with mint leaves for that extra touch of freshness.

"FAR SIDE" VANILLA AND APPLE MOUSSE

SERVES

4

APPLE PUREE

6 large apples
(such as Granny Smith, Honeycrisp, or Fuji), peeled, cored, and chopped

⅓ cup (80 ml) water

3 tbsp. (40 g) sugar
(adjust to taste)

VANILLA MOUSSE

¾ cup (170 g) cream cheese

¾ cup (150 g) sugar

2 ¼ cups (540 ml) heavy whipping cream

2 tsp. (10 g) vanilla

¼ tsp. (1.2 g) salt

After a thrilling day on the slopes, there's nothing quite like indulging in a dessert that captures the essence of the winter season. Just like the Far Side run at K3—where the snow is perfect, the runs are unforgettable, and every turn is pure magic—this apple and vanilla mousse is a hidden gem worth discovering. Fluffy vanilla mousse meets sweet, tangy apple puree in a dessert that's as light as fresh powder and as comforting as a post-ski fireside moment. Each layer is thoughtfully crafted, offering a delightful contrast of flavors and textures.

1. In a medium saucepan, cook the apples with water over medium heat, stirring occasionally, until very soft, about 15 to 20 minutes. Add a splash of water if needed. Remove from heat and blend until smooth. Stir in sugar to taste and let the puree cool completely for your layers.

2. Ensure that the cream cheese is at room temperature for easy mixing.

3. In a large bowl, whip the cream until stiff peaks form. You can use a standard mixer or a hand mixer with a whisk attachment. Set aside.

4. In a separate bowl, beat the cream cheese until it's super smooth. Add the sugar, vanilla, and a tiny pinch of salt. Keep beating until everything is perfectly blended—no lumps allowed!

5. Gently fold the whipped cream into the cream cheese mixture, taking your time to maintain that light and airy texture. Think of it like dressing for a day on the slopes—each layer is important!

6. Spoon a generous amount of apple puree into a clear glass, showcasing the beautiful color. Then, add a layer of the vanilla mousse—use a piping bag for precision or simply spoon it in gently to keep those layers distinct.

7. Alternate with more apple puree and then more vanilla mousse, repeating until you run out of ingredients. Aim for that gorgeous, layered effect, reminiscent of the stripes on a perfectly groomed ski trail. Chill in the fridge for at least an hour to let the flavors meld beautifully.

8. Just before serving, top with berries for a pop of color and freshness.

"LARRY'S" CHOCOLATE AND BERRY MOUSSE

SERVES

4

MOUNTAIN BERRY PUREE

2 cups (300 g) mixed berries (strawberries, raspberries, blackberries, blueberries)

2 tbsp. (30 g) sugar (adjust to taste)

1 tbsp. (15 ml) freshly squeezed lemon juice

CHOCOLATE MOUSSE

1 + ⅓ cups (227 g) dark chocolate (70% cocoa), cut into small pieces

3 tbsp. (43 g) unsalted butter

4 eggs, separated into yolks and whites

¼ cup (50 g) sugar, divided

1 tsp. (5 g) vanilla

¼ tsp. (1.2g) salt

1 cup (240 ml) heavy cream

This indulgent duo of rich chocolate and vibrant forest fruits is a tribute to the legendary ski run, Larry's Line—named after Larry, a K3 character from day one. This cloudlike chocolate mousse melts effortlessly in your mouth, while the berry-infused layers of puree offer a refreshing contrast. When layered together, these two elements create a harmonious blend of textures and flavors, delivering a dessert that is both indulgent and refreshing. The true beauty of this dessert lies not only in its taste but in its presentation—served in clear glasses, the layers of velvety chocolate and vibrant berry puree create a visual feast for the eyes as well as the palate.

1. Gather your berries and hull any strawberries, then wash gently. Place your berries into a medium saucepan with the sugar and lemon juice. Let them simmer over medium heat until they start to break down. Use a blender or an immersion blender and transform your berries into a silky puree. Strain through a fine mesh sieve to catch any seeds. Set aside to cool.

2. Combine the chocolate with the butter in a heatproof bowl. Place over a saucepan of simmering water and let it melt gently. Stir until smooth and shiny.

3. In a separate bowl, whisk the egg yolks with half the sugar until the mixture is light and creamy. Add the vanilla, bringing a cozy lodge warmth to the mousse. Gently whisk this into the melted chocolate mixture.

4. In a separate bowl, whisk the egg whites and salt until soft peaks form. Gradually add the remaining sugar, beating until firm, snowy peaks form. Gently fold one-third of the egg whites into the chocolate mixture to lighten it, then carefully fold in the rest, maintaining the mousse's airy texture.

5. In another separate bowl, whip the cream until soft peaks form, then fold it into the chocolate mixture using gentle strokes. Aim for a mousse as smooth as freshly groomed slopes.

6 Using four clear glasses or ramekins, start with a layer of chocolate mousse, followed by a layer of berry puree. Repeat this process, creating layers until you fill the glasses, ending with a top layer of chocolate mousse. You can use a piping bag to layer the mousse neatly if you want a more polished presentation.

7 Cover and refrigerate for at least two hours, allowing the dessert to set.

8 Top with berries and a dollop of whipped cream before serving for a fresh and vibrant contrast to the mousse.

"NOTHING LEFT"
CHOCOLATE LAYER CAKE

SERVES

10–12

CAKE

2 cups (240 g) all-purpose flour

½ tsp. (2.5 g) baking soda

½ tsp. (2 g) baking powder

1 ¾ cups (350 g) light brown sugar

¾ cup (75 g) cocoa powder

½ tsp. (2.5 g) salt

2 eggs

½ cup (120 ml) milk

½ cup (120 g) yogurt

½ cup (120 ml) olive oil

1 tbsp. (15 ml) vanilla essence

1 ½ cups (360 ml) brewed coffee (cooled)

CAKE FILLING

1 cup (150 g) dark chocolate, chopped into small pieces

1 cup (150 g) milk chocolate, chopped into small pieces

1 cup (227 g) unsalted butter, at room temperature

2 tsp. (10 g) vanilla

½ cup (115 g) cream cheese

GANACHE

1 cup (240 ml) heavy cream

1 ½ cups (225 g) dark chocolate

"NOTHING LEFT" CHOCOLATE LAYER CAKE

"Nothing Left" Chocolate Layer Cake—steep, smooth, and decadently bold. Inspired by the legendary K3 run, this cake packs the intensity of the mountain itself. Layers of ultra-moist chocolate cake are enveloped in a glossy, velvety ganache that melts effortlessly in your mouth. Rich, deep, and smooth—until you encounter a delightful crunch, reminiscent of those sneaky stumps that keep you on your toes. Each bite is an adventure, thrilling and unforgettable, just like carving down Nothing Left: fast and exhilarating. And if you're hoping for leftovers after a day on the slopes, good luck—by the time you're back, there's usually nothing left!

1. Preheat the oven to 350°F (175°C). While that's heating up, grease three 8-inch (20 cm) cake tins and line the bottoms with parchment paper.

2. In a large bowl, sift together the flour, baking soda, baking powder, brown sugar, cocoa, and salt. Give them a good whisk to mix everything evenly.

3. In a separate bowl, whisk together the eggs, milk, yogurt, olive oil, and vanilla until smooth. Slowly stir in the cooled coffee.

4. Gradually pour the wet ingredients into the dry ingredients, whisking gently until you have a smooth, glossy batter. Be careful not to overmix—just combine until no streaks of flour remain.

5. Pour the batter into your prepared tins and pop them in the oven. Bake for about 15 to 20 minutes, or until a toothpick inserted in the middle comes out clean. When the cakes are done, let them cool in the pans for about 10 minutes, then turn them out onto a wire rack to cool completely.

6. While the cakes cool, melt the dark and milk chocolate in a double boiler over medium heat until it's smooth and glossy. Let it cool slightly while you continue. In a large bowl, beat the butter until it's smooth and creamy. An electric mixer on medium speed works wonders here. Add the cream cheese and beat together until fully combined and smooth. Don't forget the vanilla—mix it in well—then fold in the cooled chocolate. Set the filling aside.

7   In a small saucepan, heat the cream over medium heat until just before it reaches the scalding point. Pour the hot cream over the chocolate and let it rest for about 3 minutes, allowing the chocolate to soften. After the resting period, stir gently with a whisk or spatula until you achieve a smooth, glossy consistency. All chocolate should be melted and well combined. Set aside.

8   Place the first cake layer on a serving plate. Evenly spread one-third of the filling over this layer. Add the second cake layer on top and spread another third of the filling. Place the final cake layer on top and use the remaining filling to thinly spread over the top and smooth out the sides for a clean finish.

9   Refrigerate the cake for about 15 minutes to allow the filling to firm up, ensuring a neat and solid finish.

10 Slowly pour the warm chocolate ganache over the entire cake, using a large metal icing spatula to smooth it into a perfect finish.

11 Carefully transfer the cake onto a serving plate and pop it into the fridge to set for several hours.

CINNAMON APPLE CARAMEL CAKE

SERVES

10

CAKE

5 large apples
(such as Granny Smith or Honeycrisp),
peeled, cored, and sliced

1 tbsp. (7.5 g) ground cinnamon

5 tbsp. (75 g) sugar

4 eggs,
at room temperature

2 cups (400 g) white caster sugar

1 cup (240 ml) neutral oil,
such as avocado, sunflower,
or canola—pick your favorite

2 tsp. (5 g) vanilla

½ cup (120 ml) freshly squeezed
orange juice (this adds a lovely zesty flavor)

3 cups (360 g) all-purpose flour

1 tbsp. (12 g) baking powder

CARAMEL SAUCE

⅓ cup (76 g) unsalted butter

¾ cup (150 g) sugar

½ tsp. (2.5 g) salt

3 tbsp. (45 ml) cream

There is always room for one more apple dessert, and this apple cake is a true ski lodge classic—humble, a little rustic, and completely irresistible. I must have dozens of apple dessert recipes stashed away, but this one always finds its way back into the rotation. And as for the caramel drizzle on top? That's just me being a little extra. It adds a buttery richness that makes each bite feel like a treat—especially when served warm with a scoop of vanilla or a big mug of something cozy. This one's for Rich, one of our longtime ski guides. When he's not charging through fresh powder, you'll find him back at the lodge, sipping coffee and sneaking another slice. He claims it's for "fuel"—we're not here to argue.

1. Preheating the oven to 350°F (175°C). Grease and line a 9-inch (23 cm) springform pan.

2. Slice the apples into sturdy segments. You want a bit of thickness here, so they hold up and give you that tender bite after baking. Toss the slices with a good shake of cinnamon and sugar—think of it as a cinnamon blanket they'll soak up! Let them sit to absorb that sweet-spicy magic while you move on to the batter.

3. In a large bowl, crack your eggs and whisk them with the sugar until smooth and just a touch pale. Slowly stream in the oil as you whisk. Add the vanilla and a splash of orange juice—just the right burst of flavor to balance out the cinnamon apples.

4. In a separate bowl, whisk together the flour and baking powder to make sure they're fully blended (no surprise baking powder lumps!). Gently fold this dry mix into the wet ingredients, taking care not to overmix. Think "gentle swoops" rather than a full workout; we want a tender, fluffy crumb!

5. Pour half the batter into your prepared pan. Now, layer half of those sweet, cinnamon-coated apples on top, as if you're tucking little apple slices under a warm batter blanket. Pour the rest of the batter over them, then artfully arrange the remaining apple slices on top for a caramelized finish.

6   Bake the cake for 60 to 70 minutes. Peek at it with a toothpick when the timer's up; if it comes out clean, it's ready. The top should have a little crunch, and the apples will have melted into the batter for pockets of caramelized apple goodness. Let the cake cool in the pan for 10 to 15 minutes before removing it.

7   In a medium saucepan, melt the butter over medium heat. Add the sugar and salt, stirring continuously until the sugar dissolves and the mixture becomes smooth and starts to bubble.

8   Once the sugar has melted and the mixture is smooth, carefully add the cream. It will bubble up, so be cautious! Stir the mixture until it thickens and becomes glossy.

9   Let the caramel sauce simmer for 1 to 2 minutes until it thickens slightly (you can test it by dipping a spoon into the sauce—it should coat the back of the spoon).

10 Remove from the heat and allow the sauce to cool for a few minutes before drizzling it over your apple cake. The warm caramel will soak into the cake slightly and add a rich, decadent layer of flavor.

**CINNAMON APPLE
CARAMEL CAKE**

"12 BEARS" APPLE BERRY STREUSEL PIE

SERVES
10

CRUST

1 + ¾ cups (220 g) all-purpose flour

1 tsp. (5 g) salt

¾ cup (170 g) unsalted butter, chilled and cut into cubes

4–6 tbsp. (60–80 ml) iced water

APPLE AND BERRY FILLING

6–7 apples
(such as Granny Smith or Honeycrisp), peeled, cored, and sliced

1 cup (200 g) sugar

¼ cup (50 g) light brown sugar

½ tsp. (2.5 g) salt

1 tsp. (5 g) ground cinnamon

3 tbsp. (45 ml) water

3 tbsp. (25 g) cornstarch

1 tbsp. (14 g) unsalted butter

2 cups (300 g) fresh berries
(blackberries, raspberries, blueberries)

WALNUT STREUSEL TOPPING

½ cup (60 g) all-purpose flour

¼ cup (50 g) brown sugar

2 tbsp. (28 g) unsalted butter, chilled and cut into cubes

½ cup (60 g) walnuts, chopped

1 tsp. (5 g) ground cinnamon

We originally dreamed of making this pie with huckleberries—after all, bears love them, and so do we! But since they can be tricky to find, we've swapped them for blueberries, keeping that same burst of tart-sweet flavor in every bite. This delightful pie, inspired by the rugged beauty of the 12 Bears run at K3, brings together sweet apples and tangy berries for a filling that's both rich and refreshing. Topped with a buttery walnut streusel, it delivers the perfect contrast of crunch and tenderness. With warm spices, juicy fruit, and a nutty crunch, every bite is a celebration of winter's finest flavors.

1. In a large bowl, combine the flour and salt. Toss in the butter and use a pastry cutter or your fingertips to blend until the mixture resembles coarse breadcrumbs. (For a speedy option, you can toss everything into a food processor and pulse until just combined.)

2. Next, add the ice-cold water—1 tablespoon at a time—mixing gently until the dough just comes together. Form the dough into a flat disk, wrap it in plastic, and pop it in the fridge for at least an hour.

3. In a saucepan, combine the apples, sugars, salt, and cinnamon Cook over medium to high heat, uncovered, for about 8 to 10 minutes, stirring occasionally to avoid any sticky situations. We want those apples soft but not mushy.

4. Now, grab a cup and whisk together the cold water and cornstarch until smooth. Pour this mixture into the pan with the apples and cook for another minute until bubbly. Stir gently until the sauce thickens and coats the fruit. Take off the heat and stir in the butter for that luxurious finish.

5. Pour the apple mixture into a shallow bowl and let it cool. Once it's at a perfect temperature, gently fold in the berries.

6. In the bowl of a food processor, combine the flour, brown sugar, butter, walnuts, and cinnamon. Pulse until coarse crumbs form. Set aside for later.

7   Preheat the oven to 375°F (190°C). Roll out the chilled dough on a lightly floured surface until it's about 12 inches (30 cm) in diameter. Gently transfer it into a 9-inch (23 cm) pie dish, pressing it into the corners without stretching it. Trim any excess pastry, leaving a lovely overhang. Prick the surface with a fork and let it chill for another 15 minutes. To keep the crust from getting soggy, partially bake it before filling it, a process called baking blind.

8   Pour the apple and berry mixture into the crust, spreading it out evenly. Now, sprinkle the walnut streusel topping generously over the top. Place the pie on a baking sheet (to catch any delicious drips) and pop it into the oven. Bake for 50 to 60 minutes or until the topping is golden brown and the filling is bubbly.

9   Once done, let the pie cool on a wire rack for about 2 hours to set that filling. Serve it warm with a scoop of vanilla or chocolate ice cream, a dollop of whipped cream, or just as it is—because this pie is a star all on its own!

CARROT COCONUT CAKE WITH WHITE CHOCOLATE FROSTING

SERVES 10

CAKE

3 cups (360 g) all-purpose flour

2 tsp. (10 g) baking soda

2 tsp. (8 g) baking powder

1 ½ tsp. (7.5 g) ground cinnamon

¼ tsp. (1.2 g) salt

1 cup (200 g) white sugar

1 cup (220 g) brown sugar

4 eggs

1 + ¼ cups (300 ml) coconut oil, at room temperature

2 tsp. (10 g) vanilla essence

3 cups (360 g) shredded carrots

1 + ½ cups (180 g) almonds, coarsely chopped

2 cups (180 g) flaked coconut

WHITE CHOCOLATE FROSTING (BECAUSE LIFE IS BETTER WITH FROSTING)

1 cup (270 g) cream cheese, firm, not spreadable

¼ cup (57 g) unsalted butter, at room temperature

1 tbsp. (15 ml) vanilla extract

½ cup (90 g) white chocolate

3 cups (360 g) powdered sugar, sifted

This carrot cake is more than just dessert—it's a little slice of tropical escape right in the heart of the mountains. I use coconut oil for a subtle island vibe, along with a blend of white and brown sugar to keep it sweet but balanced—just enough to lift your spirits without leading to a sugar crash. Leftovers (when there are any!) tend to vanish into the lunch boxes of the guides. Shelby, one of our cat drivers, has a knack for showing up right when it's fresh out of the oven. When she's not navigating the snowcat through blizzards or blasting her favorite classic rock tunes in the cab, she's sneaking a second slice and grinning like she's won the lottery. For Shelby, this cake isn't just dessert—it's the best part of the day.

1. Preheat the oven to 350°F (175°C). Grab your trusty 10-inch (26 cm) springform pan, give it a good grease, and line the bottom with parchment paper.

2. In a large bowl, sift together the flour, baking soda, baking powder, cinnamon, and salt. Next, toss in the white and brown sugars, making sure there are no sneaky lumps hiding in the brown sugar.

3. In a separate bowl, whisk the eggs until they're just beaten, then stir in the coconut oil and vanilla until combined.

4. Gently mix the dry ingredients into the wet mixture until just combined but not overmixed.

5. Fold in the carrots, almonds, and coconut, making sure they're well distributed throughout the batter. This is where all the flavor and texture come alive!

6. Pour the batter into your prepared pan and send it off to the oven for about 45 to 50 minutes. You'll know it's done when a toothpick inserted in the center comes out clean. Let the cake chill in the pan for about 10 minutes, then turn it out onto a wire rack to cool completely.

7. While the cake cools, beat the cream cheese in a large bowl until smooth and creamy. Add in the butter and a splash of vanilla, blending until it's all perfectly combined.

8   Melt the white chocolate using a double boiler over medium heat—this will give you that silky texture we're after. Once melted, pour it into the cream cheese mixture and mix it until everything is smooth. Gradually add the powdered sugar, 1 cup at a time, beating well after each addition until your frosting is fluffy.

9   Spread the white chocolate frosting generously over the cooled carrot cake, letting it cascade down the sides. Slice it up, serve, and enjoy the cozy flavors.

SERVES

8–10

PASTRY

1 + ½ cups (187 g) all-purpose flour

3 tbsp. (42 g) sugar

¼ tsp. (1.2 g) fine salt

½ cup (250 g) cold butter, unsalted and cut into small pieces

5–7 tbsp. (75–100 ml) iced water

BLUEBERRY FILLING

¼ cup (50 g) sugar

1 tbsp. (8 g). cornstarch

1 tsp. (2 g) lemon zest

¼ tsp. (1.2 g) ground cinnamon

1/8 tsp. (.75 g) salt

3 cups (280 g) fresh blueberries (do not use frozen)

2 tsp. (10 g) freshly squeezed lemon juice

CRUMBLE

¼ cup (30 g) all-purpose flour

¼ cup (130 g) almonds, chopped

¼ cup (50 g) brown sugar

¼ cup (25 g) rolled oats

CHOCOLATE CARAMEL SAUCE

1 cup (200 g) sugar

2 tbsp. (30 ml) water

¼ cup (57 g) unsalted butter, cubed

½ cup (120 ml) heavy cream, warmed

3 oz. (85 g) dark chocolate (70% cocoa), finely chopped

½ tsp. (2.5 g) vanilla extract

Flaky sea salt (optional, for a salted twist)

"SALLY'S HUCK" BLUEBERRY TART WITH CHOCOLATE CARAMEL SAUCE

Nothing warms the soul quite like a slice of blueberry tart—just ask Sally. One frosty morning, she and her dad set out to explore a new line. Sally launched off a jump near the bottom and landed perfectly, feeling on top of the world. Later, after the group wrapped up their avalanche training and repeated the run, she hit that same jump a second time—and landed right in the hole from her first attempt. The result? A perfect collision between her knee and chin. There were tears, but Sally eventually laughed it off. The group couldn't resist naming the run after her, a lasting tribute to her double feature in the same hole. But hey, her bruised ego needed serious soothing, and nothing does that better than a warm, buttery tart.

PASTRY

1 In the bowl of a food processor, combine the flour, sugar, and salt. Pulse a few times until just mixed. Add the butter and pulse again until the mixture resembles coarse breadcrumbs, with small bits of butter still visible—these bits are the secret to a flaky crust! Gradually add the cold water, pulsing gently until the dough just begins to come together. Remember, rustic means simplicity—don't overwork it!

2 Turn the dough out onto a lightly floured surface and knead it gently until well combined. It will be crumbly at first but will come together beautifully. Shape the dough into a disk, wrap it in plastic wrap, and refrigerate for at least 30 minutes.

3 Preheat the oven to 400°F (200°C). Line a baking sheet with parchment paper for easy cleanup.

4 On a lightly floured surface, roll out the chilled dough into a roughly 12-inch (30 cm) circle. Remember, perfection isn't the goal—embracing the rustic look adds to its charm!

BLUEBERRY FILLING

5 In a medium bowl, combine the sugar, cornstarch, lemon zest, cinnamon, and salt. Gently fold in the blueberries and lemon juice, allowing the flavors to meld.

6   Place the blueberry mixture in the center of the rolled-out dough, leaving a 2-inch (6 cm) border around the edges. Carefully fold the edges of the dough over the filling, pleating as you go to create a lovely, free-form tart.

CRUMBLE

7   In a medium bowl, mix the flour, almonds, brown sugar, and rolled oats. Fold in the butter until the mixture resembles coarse breadcrumbs. This topping adds a crunch to your tart. Sprinkle the crumble mixture evenly over the blueberry filling.

8   Transfer the tart to the prepared baking sheet and bake in the oven for 35 to 40 minutes, or until the crust is golden brown and the filling is bubbling.

9   Allow the tart to cool slightly before slicing.

CHOCOLATE CARAMEL SAUCE

10 In a medium saucepan over medium heat, combine the sugar and water. Stir gently until the sugar dissolves, then stop stirring. Let it simmer until the mixture turns a deep amber color (about 6 to 8 minutes).

11 Carefully whisk in the butter, one cube at a time. It will bubble vigorously—don't panic, that's caramel magic at work!

12 Slowly whisk in the warm cream until smooth and glossy. If any caramel seizes up, keep stirring over low heat until it melts back down.

13 Remove the saucepan from the heat and stir in the dark chocolate until completely melted and silky.

14 Stir in the vanilla, and a pinch of salt if you're feeling fancy.

15 Serve with a dollop of whipped cream or a scoop of ice cream for an extra touch of indulgence. And if you really want to turn up the decadence, drizzle a little chocolate caramel sauce on the side—because sometimes, a second helping is as irresistible as a second lap through the same bomb hole (hopefully with a smoother landing the third time around).

MOUNTAIN MORSELS: A LITTLE BIT OF EVERYTHING

Mountain Morsels is the catchall cabin for the recipes that don't quite follow the trail—but still deserve a spot by the fire. From steamy drinks to off-the-map snacks, these are the little comforts that complete the alpine experience. And yes, there's hot chocolate.

SERVES

4

2-inch (5 cm) piece of fresh gingerroot

4 cups (960 ml) water

Zest of 1 lemon or orange
(or both for extra citrusy flair!)

1 tbsp. (15 ml) honey, agave,
or maple syrup (your choice!)

Extra lemon or orange juice
for a tangy kick (optional)

GINGER GLOW TEA

I started making this tea for guests who, after the twists and turns of the snowcat ride, often felt a bit uneasy from the motion. This warming, spicy brew works wonders to settle your stomach and calm any motion sickness from the ride. Ginger is known for its natural ability to ease nausea. Not only does it help balance out the motion, but it's packed with antioxidants and anti-inflammatory properties that also help ease any muscle soreness after a day on the slopes.

1. Peel the ginger and either grate it or chop it into small pieces. The finer you chop or grate, the more potent the tea will be.

2. In a medium pot, bring the water to a boil.

3. Toss the ginger into the boiling water. Add the zest of your chosen citrus (or both for an extra pop of flavor). Let it all bubble away for 10 to 15 minutes, depending on how strong you like it.

4. Once you've got that perfect ginger infusion, sweeten it to taste with honey, agave, or maple syrup. Stir in a little or a lot—it's up to you!

5. Strain out the ginger pieces and citrus zest, then pour the tea into four cups. Add a splash of lemon or orange juice for an extra citrus punch if you like.

"HAPPY ENDING" HOT CHOCOLATE

SERVES

4

4 cups (1 L) whole milk

½ cup (120 ml) heavy cream

½ cup (100 g) dark chocolate, chopped

2 tbsp. (10 g) unsweetened cocoa powder

2 tbsp. (25 g) sugar (or to taste)

½ tsp. (2.5 g) vanilla extract

¼ tsp. (1.2 g) ground cinnamon

Whipped cream or marshmallows, for topping

OPTIONAL ADD-ONS

1 shot (30 ml) Baileys, spiced rum, or peppermint schnapps per serving

There's nothing quite like wrapping your hands around a steaming mug of hot chocolate after a day on the slopes—much like the feeling of cruising down the Happy Ending run at K3, where you're delighted to be back at the lodge. This isn't just any hot chocolate; it's a ski-lodge-style hug in a mug. Rich, creamy, and chocolatey, this recipe will have you swapping stories by the fireplace and reaching for seconds.

The secret? A mix of dark chocolate and cocoa powder for depth, a pinch of cinnamon for a cozy twist, and a splash of heavy cream to make it luxuriously silky. Top it off with whipped cream, marshmallows, or even a drizzle of caramel if you're feeling fancy. Oh, and if you're looking for an adults-only après-ski treat, a shot of Baileys or spiced rum turns this into pure alpine magic.

1. In a medium saucepan over medium heat, combine the milk and heavy cream. Warm until steaming but not boiling.

2. Stir in the dark chocolate, cocoa powder, and sugar. Whisk until the chocolate is completely melted and the mixture is smooth.

3. Stir in the vanilla and cinnamon for that extra kick.

4. Pour into four mugs, top with whipped cream or marshmallows, and dust with a pinch of cocoa powder or cinnamon for flair.

5. If you want to make it boozy, stir the alcohol in before topping with the whipped cream or marshmallows.

CANADIAN LODGE GRANOLA

SERVES

4

2 cups (200 g) rolled oats

½ cup (60 g) pecans, chopped

½ cup (60 g) flaked almonds

¼ cup (25 g) sunflower seeds

¼ cup (30 g) pumpkin seeds

½ tsp. (2.5 g) cinnamon

¼ tsp. (1.2 g) salt

¼ cup (60 ml) pure maple syrup

2 tbsp. (30 ml) coconut oil or melted butter

1 tsp. (2.5 g) vanilla extract

½ cup (75 g) dried cranberries or raisins

¼ cup (40 g) shredded coconut

¼ cup (40 g) hempseeds

2 tsp. (2 g) finely grated orange zest

I've crafted all kinds of granolas over the years—each one shaped by where I am in the world, using seasonal and local ingredients. In the Caribbean, its mango, coconut, and cashews. In the Alps, its mountain honey, hearty grains, and toasted hazelnuts.

But this one is made for the Monashee's. Built for snowy mornings and high-altitude hunger, it's packed with rolled oats, crunchy nuts, tart dried cranberries, and a generous drizzle of rich Canadian maple syrup. Pumpkin seeds bring an earthy bite, and a hint of cinnamon warms every spoonful. Simple, rugged, and full of character—just like the mountains that inspired it.

1. Preheat the oven to 325°F (165°C) and line a large baking sheet with parchment paper.

2. In a large bowl, combine the oats, pecans, almonds, sunflower seeds, pumpkin seeds, cinnamon, and salt.

3. In a small saucepan or microwave-safe bowl, warm the maple syrup and coconut oil until melted and combined. Stir in the vanilla.

4. Pour the wet mixture over the dry ingredients and mix well until everything is evenly coated.

5. Spread the mixture onto the prepared baking sheet in an even layer. Bake for 20 to 25 minutes, stirring halfway through, until golden and fragrant.

6. Remove from the oven and immediately stir in the dried cranberries (and coconut, if using) and orange zest. Allow the granola to cool completely on the baking sheet—it will crisp up as it cools.

7. Serve with yogurt and fruit or pack it into airtight containers for a quick lodge breakfast or trail snack.

"KRIS'S COOKIES": THE SNOWCAT'S FAVORITE CHOCOLATE CHIP TREAT

MAKES
24–30 COOKIES

1 cup (227 g) unsalted butter, at room temperature

1 cup (212 g) light brown sugar, packed

½ cup (99 g) white sugar

2 eggs, at room temperature

2 tsp. (10 g) vanilla extract

2 + ⅓ cups (270 g) all-purpose flour

½ tsp. (2 g) baking powder

1 tsp. (5 g) baking soda

1 tsp. (5 g) ground cinnamon

2 cups (340 g) chocolate chunks (because chips are too small)

1 tsp. (5 g) flaky sea salt

Ever wonder what fuels the snowcat on its chilly mountain missions? It's not just the engine—it's Kris's Cookies! Named after Kris, the snowcat crew's biggest cookie fan, these chewy, gooey chocolate chip treats quickly became a favorite. Bursting with melty chocolate and cozy snowy-day comfort, they've earned their spot as the unofficial snack of the slopes.

1. Preheat the oven to 350°F (175°C). Line two baking sheets with parchment paper or silicone mats, because nobody likes cookies that stick! This way, you can just pop them off with ease.

2. In a large bowl, beat the butter until it's soft and smooth. Add the light brown and white sugars and whisk until the mixture is creamy. Mix in the eggs until fully combined, then stir in the vanilla.

3. In a separate bowl, whisk together the flour, baking soda, cinnamon, and salt. These are the building blocks for your perfect cookie base!

4. Slowly add the dry ingredients to the wet ingredients, stirring gently. No need to rush—mix until everything is just combined and your dough is soft and smooth.

5. Gently fold in the chocolate chunks—don't be shy about sneaking a few. Stir until every bite promises a burst of rich, chocolatey goodness.

6. Use a cookie scoop or a spoon to drop dollops of dough onto your prepared baking sheets, spacing them about 2 inches apart. These cookies will spread, so give them a little room to breathe!

7. Bake the cookies for 10 to 12 minutes, or until the edges are golden and the centers are still a little soft. Trust the smell—you'll know when they're close!

8. Let the cookies cool on the baking sheets for 5 minutes before transferring them to a wire rack to cool completely. Or, if you're like me, just eat them while they're still warm and gooey.

K3 GRANOLA BARS

MAKES
12–16 BARS

1 + ⅔ cups (150 g) quick oats

⅓ cup (40 g) all-purpose flour

¼ tsp. (1.2 g) salt

1 tsp. (5 g) ground cinnamon

1 cup (100 g) whole pecans

1 cup (150 g) mixed dried fruit

1 cup (100 g) whole walnuts

⅓ cup (40 g) peanut butter, at room temperature

1 tsp. (5 g) vanilla

¾ cup (150 g) brown sugar

⅓ cup (75 g) melted butter

⅓ cup (112 g) honey

2 tbsp. (30 ml) maple syrup

1–2 tbsp. (15–30 ml) water

Not your average granola bar! These crunchy, chewy, and nutty treats are a favorite of our lodge guests and staff alike. We pack them in the snowcat lunch coolers, where they get a good jolt on the cat roads—making them taste even better by the time you dig in! Packed with creamy peanut butter, roasted nuts, and dried fruit, these bars are the ultimate snack to keep you going all day. Perfect for a quick bite on the slopes or a satisfying nibble at the lodge, they're the ideal companion for every adventure!

1. Preheat the oven to 350°F (175°C). Line an 8 x 8-inch (20 x 20 cm) square pan with two pieces of parchment paper, extending up the sides to create a sling—this will make it easy to lift the bars out later.

2. In a large bowl, combine the oats, flour, salt, cinnamon, pecans, dried fruit, and walnuts. Give everything a thorough toss until all the ingredients are evenly distributed.

3. In a separate bowl, whisk together the peanut butter, vanilla, brown sugar, melted butter, honey, maple syrup, and water. Whisk until smooth and glossy, ensuring every bit is well incorporated.

4. Pour the wet mixture over the dry ingredients. Stir well, until every oat, nut, and piece of fruit is coated and the mixture looks thick and delicious.

5. Transfer the mixture into your prepared pan. Press it firmly into the corners and smooth the top with a spatula or your hands. (The firmer you press, the better the bars will hold together!)

6. Bake the bars for 25 to 30 minutes, until the top is golden and the edges are a shade darker. Your kitchen will smell incredible!

7. Allow the bars to cool completely in the pan. Then, use the parchment sling to lift them out and place on a cutting board. Using a sharp serrated knife, cut into the bars with a gentle sawing motion to keep them intact.

MACKENZIE'S MAC AND CHEESE

SERVES
4

1 lb. (450 g) elbow macaroni

2 cups (480 ml) whole milk

1 cup (240 ml) heavy cream

¼ cup (57 g) unsalted butter

¼ cup (30 g) all-purpose flour

1 tsp. (5 g) Dijon mustard (optional, for a subtle tang)

2 cups (200 g) shredded sharp cheddar cheese

1 cup (100 g) shredded Gruyère cheese (for a rich, nutty flavor)

Sea salt and freshly ground black pepper to taste

½ cup (50 g) panko breadcrumbs (for a crispy topping)

Chopped fresh parsley (for garnish)

Comfort food at its peak! Named after Mackenzie—one of our favorite tail guides, who rides with the biggest smile and the warmest vibes—this creamy, cheesy classic is a lodge essential and an undeniable crowd-pleaser. Whether you're thawing out after a powder day or gathering for a family-style feast, this mac and cheese always delivers. It may not shred the slopes like Mackenzie, but it's just as dependable—and no après-ski spread is complete without it.

1. Bring a large pot of salted water to a boil and cook the pasta according to the package directions until al dente; don't overdo it or you will end up with mushy macaroni instead of cheesy perfection. Drain and set aside.

2. For a smoother sauce, gently warm the milk and cream in a small saucepan or the microwave—this helps the roux come together without lumps.

3. In a medium saucepan, melt the butter over medium heat. Add the flour and whisk constantly to form a roux (a smooth paste). Cook for 1 to 2 minutes until golden and bubbly.

4. Slowly pour in the warm milk and cream, whisking continuously to prevent lumps. Cook, stirring often, until the mixture thickens—about 5 minutes.

5. Stir in the Dijon mustard (if using) and the cheddar and Gruyère cheeses. Keep stirring until the cheese is fully melted, and the sauce is smooth and creamy. Season with salt and pepper to taste.

6. In a 2.5- to 3-quart (2.5 to 3 L) ovenproof casserole dish, combine the cooked macaroni with the cheese sauce. Stir until every noodle is coated. Season with salt and pepper to taste.

7. Sprinkle the panko breadcrumbs evenly over the top for a golden, crunchy finish.

8. Preheat the oven to 375°F (190°C) and bake uncovered for 15 to 20 minutes, or until the top is crisp and golden.

9. Garnish with parsley (if desired).

CHILLED AND FILLED: SNOWCAT SANDWICHES

These sandwiches are the perfect fuel for a day on the go, made fresh first thing after breakfast and packed in the cooler for the whole day. Built with hearty, dense bread, they hold up beautifully—even when the cat is bouncing over rugged cat roads. With two filling options to choose from, you can enjoy a Shredded Chicken with Basil Mayonnaise or a Roast Beef or Ham with Caper-Gerkin Cream Cheese Spread. Since the snowcat doesn't stop for lunch, these sandwiches are designed to be easy to eat on the move, keeping the cat skiers energized and ready to tackle the slopes without missing a beat.

SERVES

2

BASIL MAYONNAISE

¼ cup (60 g) mayonnaise

1 tbsp. (5 g) finely chopped fresh basil

1 tsp. (5 g) freshly squeezed lemon juice

Sea salt and freshly ground black pepper to taste

CHICKEN SANDWICH

4 slices of dense bread (sourdough, rye, or multigrain)

1 ½ cups (225 g) shredded cooked chicken (rotisserie works great)

⅓ cup (80 g) basil mayonnaise

2 large leaves of crisp lettuce (like Romaine or butterhead)

SHREDDED CHICKEN SANDWICH WITH BASIL MAYONNAISE

1. Mix the mayonnaise, basil, lemon juice, salt, and pepper in a small bowl until smooth.

2. Lightly toast the bread slices (optional) for sturdiness and flavor.

3. In a medium bowl, combine the chicken with the basil mayonnaise and mix until evenly coated.

4. Place a leaf of lettuce on two slices of bread. Spread the chicken mixture evenly on top of the lettuce. Top with the remaining bread slices.

5. Wrap tightly in parchment or foil to keep fresh and portable.

ROAST BEEF OR HAM SANDWICH WITH CAPER-GHERKIN CREAM CHEESE SPREAD

SERVES 2

CAPER-GHERKIN CREAM CHEESE SPREAD

⅓ cup (75 g) cream cheese, at room temperature

1 tbsp. (15 g) chopped gherkins (or dill pickles)

1 tsp. (3 g) capers, finely chopped

1 tsp. (5 g) Dijon mustard

1 tsp. (5 g) freshly squeezed lemon juice

Pinch of sea salt and freshly ground black pepper

ROAST BEEF OR HAM SANDWICH

4 slices of rye or pumpernickel bread

⅓ cup (80 g) caper-gherkin cream cheese spread

4–6 slices of roast beef or ham

Baby spinach or arugula, for a fresh crunch

1. In a small bowl, mix the cream cheese, gherkins, capers, Dijon mustard, lemon juice, salt, and pepper until smooth.

2. Spread the cream cheese mixture evenly on all four slices of bread. Layer the roast beef or ham on two slices. Add baby spinach or arugula for freshness. Top with the remaining bread slices.

3. Wrap tightly in parchment paper or foil for easy transport.

TIM'S THAI BEEF SALAD WITH RICE

Bread can get a little heavy when it's your daily go-to, which is why this Thai beef salad with rice is a refreshing and satisfying alternative to sandwiches. It's light, flavorful, and an ideal way to make the most of leftover steak from dinner. Tim—one of our mountain guides—is big on protein and always chasing the best lines. He loved this so much he kept asking me to make it again. Now it's a regular in the ski guide lunch rotation, and solid proof that leftovers can be anything but boring.

SERVES 2

SALAD

- 1 cup (200 g) cooked basmati rice, cooled
- 2 cups (50 g) mixed greens (such as arugula, spinach, or baby kale)
- 1 cup (150 g) cherry tomatoes, halved
- ½ cucumber, thinly sliced
- 1 small red onion, thinly sliced
- 1 carrot, julienned or grated
- Fresh cilantro and mint leaves (for garnish)
- 7 oz. (200 g) leftover cooked beef steak, thinly sliced
- ¼ cup (30 g) roasted peanuts, roughly chopped (optional)

DRESSING

- 2 tbsp. (35 g) sweet chili sauce
- 2 tbsp. (30 ml) freshly squeezed lime juice (about 1 lime)
- 1 tbsp. (15 ml) soy sauce
- 1 tbsp. (12 g) brown sugar or (15 ml) honey
- 1 tsp. (4 g) sesame oil
- 1 red chili, finely chopped (adjust to taste)
- 1 garlic clove, minced

1. In a small bowl, whisk together the sweet chili sauce, lime juice, soy sauce, brown sugar, sesame oil, chili, and garlic until the sugar dissolves.
2. In a large bowl, combine the rice, mixed greens, cherry tomatoes, cucumber, red onion, carrot, and herbs.
3. Pour the dressing over the salad and toss gently to coat everything evenly.
4. Fold in the leftover steak, ensuring it is evenly distributed throughout the salad.
5. Divide the salad into two lunch containers. Sprinkle with peanuts (if using) and garnish with additional cilantro and mint leaves. Add a wedge of lime for an extra zing.

APPENDIX

MIND BODY AND SNOW

WELL-BEING FOR SKIERS

Skiing is a dynamic and physically demanding sport—it calls for stamina, flexibility, and a focused mind. To truly make the most of your time on the slopes, it's important to take care of your well-being both on and off the mountain. Here are a few simple ways to enhance your experience: unplug with a digital detox, stay limber with regular stretching, fuel your body with nourishing foods, and keep a few essential nutrition tips in mind.

DIGITAL DETOX: RECONNECT WITH NATURE

One of the best ways to boost your well-being on a ski trip is to step away from screens. Skiing offers the perfect digital detox—a break from emails, social media, and constant notifications.

Surrounded by snowy peaks and quiet forests, it's easier to let your mind unwind. Being fully present reduces stress, sharpens clarity, and deepens mindfulness. Whether carving fresh tracks or enjoying the lodge's fireside warmth, take the chance to unplug and immerse yourself in the moment.

The lodge, free from TVs and digital distractions, becomes a true haven for rest—snow outside, fire crackling inside—a perfect place to trade screens for connection with nature, others, and yourself.

STRETCHING AND WARMING UP: KEEP YOUR BODY FLEXIBLE

Taking a few minutes to stretch and warm up before hitting the slopes is one of the best ways to prevent injury and improve performance. Skiing demands strength, balance, and flexibility—so preparing your body beforehand helps you move more fluidly and stay safe throughout the day.

Before You Ski, Try These Simple Stretches

- **Hip flexor stretch:** Skiing puts serious strain on your hips, especially after a long day in a ski stance. Stretching them helps maintain mobility and ease of movement.
- **Hamstring stretch:** Tight hamstrings can make your turns feel stiff and increase the risk of injury. A gentle stretch here improves range of motion and control.
- **Shoulder rolls:** Your upper body does more work than you might think, especially during quick turns and pole plants. A few shoulder rolls help loosen tension and prep you for action.

A short warm-up like this doesn't take long—but your body will thank you once you're carving down the mountain.

After Skiing

Don't skip the cooldown! Stretching after a day on the slopes helps your body recover, reduces muscle soreness, and keeps you feeling limber for tomorrow's runs.

- **Quad stretch:** Your quads do most of the heavy lifting during skiing, so give them the attention they deserve with a thorough stretch to ease tightness and tension.
- **Calf stretch:** Long days in ski boots can leave your calves tight and cramp prone. A good calf stretch helps release pressure and improve circulation.

Taking just a few minutes to stretch at the end of the day can boost flexibility, reduce stiffness, and make your overall ski experience far more comfortable.

SLEEP: THE UNSUNG HERO OF SKIING PERFORMANCE

Skiing demands energy, focus, and strength—none of which are possible if you're running on empty. That's why a good night's sleep is essential, not just for performance but for recovery too. After a full day on the mountain, your muscles need time to rebuild and your mind needs rest to stay sharp.

Tips for Better Sleep on a Ski Trip

- **Stick to a routine:** Try to wake up and go to bed at the same time each day, even on vacation. A steady rhythm helps regulate your sleep cycle and promotes deeper, more restorative rest.
- **Wind down well:** After a day of fresh air and adrenaline, ease into sleep with a calming ritual—light reading, gentle stretches, or deep breathing. Avoid screens before bed to keep your brain from revving back up.
- **Prioritize comfort:** A cozy bed, supportive pillow, and warm blanket can make all the difference. Good sleep starts with a restful environment.

Take care of your body and mind, and the mountain will reward you. Whether it's stretching, fueling up with the right foods, unplugging from tech, or simply getting enough rest, these small habits make a big impact. Ski better, feel better, and enjoy every moment—on and off the slopes.

SNOW SCIENCE AND FUN FACTS

Snow is one of nature's most captivating wonders. At its core, it's simply frozen water vapor that forms high in the atmosphere. Up there, where temperatures drop well below freezing, water vapor condenses around tiny particles like dust, eventually forming ice crystals. As these crystals fall, they grow and take on unique shapes, becoming the magical snowflakes, we all love to catch on our tongues. What makes snowflakes so special is that no two are the same. The way they form is influenced by factors like humidity and temperature at various altitudes, which gives each snowflake its distinct, intricate pattern. What's even more fascinating is that most snowflakes have six sides—this is due to the way ice molecules bond together. And since snowflakes are incredibly light and delicate, they can take hours to reach the ground, giving them ample time to develop their beautiful, one-of-a-kind shapes. But snow isn't just one thing—it comes in different forms, each with its own characteristics depending on the conditions it encounters. From fluffy powder to wet, heavy snow, each type brings its own unique beauty and experience. Snow is much more than just frozen water—it's a dynamic part of nature's ever-evolving masterpiece.

Powder Snow: The dream snow for skiers and snowboarders—light, soft, and fluffy, offering a smooth, weightless ride down the slopes.

Crust: A tough, hardened layer of snow that forms when melting and refreezing create a solid surface, often making for a less-than-ideal skiing experience.

Graupel: Often referred to as "snow pellets," these are small, soft balls of snow created when supercooled water droplets freeze onto snowflakes, giving them a round, pellet-like appearance.

Hoar frost: Beautiful, delicate, feathery ice crystals that form on cold surfaces when moisture in the air instantly freezes, creating an intricate, frost-covered coating that looks like nature's own artwork.

Snow is far more than just frozen water; it's an incredible and ever-changing part of our natural world. While ice is clear, snow appears white because the ice crystals scatter light in every direction, blending all the colors of the spectrum to create white light. However, snow can take on various colors depending on what's mixed in, such as algae or minerals. One striking example is "watermelon snow," which gets its reddish hue from algae containing a red pigment.

But snow isn't just visually captivating—it plays a vital role in our environment. Around 12% of the Earth's land is covered by snow at any given time during winter. Snow also impacts language, as different cultures have developed countless words to describe various types of snow. The Scots, for example, are said to have over four hundred words for snow, including "skelf" (a large snowflake) and "feefle" (swirling snow). The Inuit's have their own rich vocabulary, like "aqilokoq" (snow falling softly) and "piegnartoq" (snow that's great for sledding).

Beyond its cultural significance, snow serves some practical purposes. Despite its cold, snow is a fantastic insulator because of the air trapped between its flakes. This is why igloos, built entirely from snow, can stay surprisingly warm inside. Snow also has a natural cleansing effect—it helps purify the air by removing pollutants as it falls.

The science behind snow is just as fascinating. Snowballs form best when the snow is near its melting point, with a thin layer of water acting like glue to hold the snowflakes together. Snow can even shape the landscape; heavy snowfalls and avalanches can transform terrain, and over time, the pressure of accumulated snow can compress it into ice, eventually forming glaciers.

So, the next time you see a snowflake drift from the sky, remember that each one is a small, unique piece of nature's incredible story. Whether it's record-breaking snowfalls or the fascinating science behind their formation, snow has a way of captivating our imagination and connecting us to the natural world in remarkable ways.

RECORD-BREAKING SNOW EVENTS

Snowiest place on earth:
Aomori City, Japan, holds the title for the snowiest city on earth, receiving an astonishing average of 26 feet (8 m) of snow annually. The city's heavy snowfall is due to the unique weather patterns created by cold Siberian winds meeting the warm moisture from the Sea of Japan.

Biggest one-day snowfall:
In 1921, Silver Lake, Colorado, recorded a mind-blowing 75.8 inches (almost 6½ feet [2 m]) of snow in just 24 hours, setting the record for the biggest one-day snowfall in U.S. history. Imagine shoveling that much snow off your driveway!

Longest snow season:
Mount Rainier in Washington State is home to one of the longest snow seasons on earth. Due to its towering height and year-round cool temperatures, snow can be found at its higher altitudes year-round, making it a paradise for snow lovers.

Largest snowflake ever recorded:
According to the Guinness World Records, the largest snowflake ever observed was a whopping 15 inches (38 cm) wide, spotted in Montana in 1887. This giant flake was part of a unique weather event that led to some of the most dramatic snowfalls in history.

Most snow in a single season:
The record for the most snow in a single winter season goes to Mount Baker, also in Washington State, where an incredible 1,140 inches (95 feet [29 m]) of snow was recorded during the 1998–1999 season. It's hard to fathom that much snow!

MONASHEE MAGIC

CHASING THE PERFECT POWDER

This book can't fully capture the magic of K3 without shining a spotlight on the exceptional climate that makes skiing here truly unforgettable. Nestled deep in the heart of British Columbia, the Monashee Mountains deliver an experience like no other—thanks to what locals call the legendary Monashee Magic.

What makes this place so special is the perfect mix of geography, reliable snowfall, and unique weather patterns that create a deep, light, and fluffy snowpack all season long. Lofty peaks and diverse terrain set the stage for winter adventurers looking for fresh powder and epic runs.

The tenure of K3 spans roughly 15,000 hectares of prime powder territory, with most of the skiing from 7,200 to 5,000 feet (2,200 to 1,600 m), though when the snow gods really smile on us, pickups can drop as low as 4,000 (1,200 m)—opening even more terrain to explore.

The forests are filled with ancient giants—majestic balsam and spruce trees up to five hundred years old, and the grand Western red cedars found on the lower slopes—offering some of the world's most magical and sought-after tree skiing.

The Monashee Mountains boast a deep, stable snowpack that keeps the stoke alive from the first tracks to the last. Here, you'll find a little bit of everything: dreamy tree runs through a burnt forest in South Park and the Far Side, hucks and jumps off the pulse-pounding Skinny Ridge that keeps the party rocking, and the Darkside—the crown jewel—where long, creamy north-facing powder stashes abound.

Whether you're chasing fresh tracks or simply soaking in the mountain magic, this is where snow dreams come alive.

APPENDIX

CLIMBING WITH CATS

THE EVOLUTION OF CAT SKIING

Cat skiing, or snowcat skiing, has always fascinated me. It all began in the mid twentieth century when skiers started looking beyond the crowded resort slopes, chasing after untouched powder. This was closely tied to the rise of off-piste and backcountry skiing, where the adventure of getting to the snow is just as exciting as the ride down. Here's a quick look at how it all came to be.

Before snowcats, accessing those untracked, pristine powder fields meant a lot of uphill hiking. As skiing grew in popularity, people began craving more than just groomed runs—they wanted the thrill of exploring untouched, off-the-grid terrain. That's when the idea of using vehicles to reach those remote spots started to take shape. Of course, it wasn't an instant success—it took time and a bit of trial and error to figure out the right gear to make it happen!

The snowcat, a large tracked vehicle built to glide over snow, was developed around 1950, but its roots trace back to 1910, when the original prototype was created to transport gear for Robert Scott's Antarctic expedition. Over the years, snowcats have evolved a lot. Initially, they were used by ski resorts for grooming trails and accessing tricky hard-to-reach areas. It didn't take long, though, for adventurous skiers to realize these vehicles could be used to access backcountry terrain that was previously off-limits or nearly impossible to reach with traditional ski lifts.

Cat skiing really gained momentum in the 1970s. Ski resorts and independent operators realized that snowcats could be used to help advanced skiers reach untracked powder—without the hassle of long, exhausting hikes! By the 1980s, it was becoming a huge trend, especially in snowy spots like British Columbia and parts of the U.S. It took off because it offered the chance to ride pristine, untouched powder without the crowds at resorts. Who wouldn't want that? By the 1990s, cat skiing was booming. Dedicated operations popped up across North America, from the Rockies to the Sierra Nevada, and even the Alps. Snowcats weren't just functional anymore—they were upgraded with heated cabins and comfy seating, making the ride to the top nearly as fun as the descent! Fast-forward to today, and snowcat technology has only improved—smoother rides, better safety, and access to even more epic terrain. Operators now focus more on avalanche safety, offering training and top-quality gear to keep everyone safe while they're out having fun. Now cat skiing is a must for anyone seeking a backcountry adventure without the effort. It's the perfect combo of wild powder turns and easy access, and you can find it all over the world—from Canada and the U.S. to Japan and Europe. Forget lift lines—just hop in a snowcat!

CAT SKIING TERMINOLOGY

Welcome to the world of cat skiing, where the mountain speaks its own language! From "fresh tracks" that make your heart race to the secret "stash" spots hidden deep in the trees, knowing the lingo helps you embrace the full experience. Whether you're chasing powder or dodging "snow snakes," this chapter will get you up to speed with all the terms you'll need to make your cat skiing adventure feel like a natural. So, grab your gear, and let's talk snow!

Air time: The moment you're soaring through the air after launching off a natural feature like a snowbank, rock, or "pillow line"!

Alpine bowl: Wide, open, and breathtakingly beautiful, an alpine bowl is like nature's arena for skiers. It's all about big turns, endless views, and freedom to roam.

Alpine glow: That magical moment at sunset when the snow reflects the warm hues of the setting sun, turning the mountain into a breathtaking view.

Avalanche conditions: The mountain's way of saying, "Not today, buddy." When snow conditions are unstable, it's better to stay safe than to risk triggering an avalanche.

Avalanche safety gear: Gear up like a mountain superhero! Your beacon, probe, and shovel are the tools you need to stay safe when you're tackling those big, untouched runs.

Backcountry bliss: The pure joy of skiing in untouched, remote snow-covered areas far away from the groomed slopes.

Backside: Want to escape the crowds? The backside is the rebel slope—untamed, untouched, and waiting for your fearless turns.

Berms: Snowbanks or mounds, often formed by wind, that can make for thrilling banked turns when skiing or riding.

Big air: When you launch off a jump and catch some serious air, feeling like you're flying through the sky before landing in the powder below. It's a moment of pure freedom!

Blower pow: The ultimate powder! Blower pow is so light and fluffy, it sprays like magic, making every turn feel like a dream sequence.

Bluebird day: A crystal clear, sunny day after a snowstorm. Think postcard-perfect conditions for your next epic descent.

Boilerplate: The "ice rink" of the mountain! If you're up for a challenge, boilerplate snow is like trying to ski on a frozen pancake—hard, slick, and totally unforgiving.

Booster run: Feeling daring? A booster run is your ticket to steep, adrenaline-pumping terrain. It's the ski slope equivalent of stepping on the gas and flying through the powder universe.

EAT, SKI & REPEAT

Boot top: When the powder is so deep, it reaches just up to your boots, making for epic turns and a full-on powder day experience.

Breakable crust: A sneaky surface layer of snow that looks soft but can snap and collapse under your weight, turning your powder dreams into a wild ride.

Burn zone: A skier's dreamscape of haunting beauty—charred tree trunks rising from pristine powder, a stark reminder of nature's power and resilience.

Cat drop: A quick drop-off at the start of a run by the snowcat, marking the beginning of your backcountry adventure.

Cat nap: The brief snooze you steal during the slow, lurching snowcat ride back uphill. Just don't miss the view!

Chalky snow: Snow that's firm but not icy—just the perfect surface for fast runs without worrying about the snow biting back.

Chatter: Feel the buzz! Chatter is that telltale vibration when your skis meet icy patches. Not ideal, but hey, it's part of the adventure.

Choker: Snow so light and deep, it's practically choking you with delight. Expect plenty of face shots with this one!

Chowder: Forget clam chowder; this "chowder" is chopped-up powder, perfect for laid-back runs and playful turns.

Chunder: The not-so-glamorous side of skiing, where snow turns into a bumpy, mashed-up mess. But hey, it's all part of the adventure, right?

Cold smoke: That heavenly, light powder snow that you can see billowing in the air when you carve through it. It's like skiing on clouds!

Cornice: The snow-sculpted edge of glory, hanging dramatically over ridges. It's like nature daring you to take the leap—proceed with caution and style!

Corn snow: A skier's summer playground that happens when the snow melts and refreezes into crunchy, snow cone–like clumps. It's like the perfect mix of spring skiing and adventure!

Crevasse: Not your average crack! A crevasse is a glacier's hidden trap, adding a thrilling edge to alpine skiing. Spotting one makes you feel like a real backcountry explorer.

Death cookies: Icy chunks of snow that make smooth runs ... not so smooth. Watch out for these sneaky little surprises!

Double eject: When both skis pop off during a wipeout. It's dramatic, hilarious, and a guaranteed crowd-pleaser.

Drop: A thrilling, often steep section of the mountain where you launch into a fresh run. It's like diving.

Dumping: When snow is falling so hard, you might need a snorkel. Translation: a powder day jackpot!

Face: No makeup needed—this "face" is all mountain. Whether steep and daunting or smooth and inviting, it's the heart of your skiing adventure, waiting to be conquered.

Face-plant: The inevitable result of hitting a deep powder patch face-first. Sometimes it's messy, but it's always memorable!

Face shots: Nature's way of saying, "Congratulations, you found the good stuff!" Skiing through deep powder sprays snow into your face—messy, glorious proof you're living the dream.

Farming turns: Precise, evenly spaced turns down a slope, resembling rows in a field. Extra satisfying to look back at your "work"!

Flat light: When the sky plays tricks on your eyes, flat light Makes every bump and slope look like a blank white canvas—thrilling and mysterious!

Flotation devices: The nickname for fat skis or wide snowboards designed for surfing the deep stuff. Float on, baby!

Fluff day: A skier's dream day when fresh, fluffy snow falls in abundance, turning the mountain into a powder paradise. It's a celebration of all things soft and dreamy.

Free refills: When snow keeps falling, covering tracks run after run. It's the gift that keeps on giving!

Freshies: First tracks in untouched snow and the ultimate prize in powder skiing. It's like skiing on clouds—soft, silent, and sublime.

Fresh tracks: The holy grail of powder skiing—those unskied, untouched lines that make your heart race with excitement. It's like you're the first one to discover a secret snow world.

Glades: Nature's obstacle course, with perfectly spaced trees and silky powder. It's like skiing through an enchanted forest—watch out for low branches!

Hero snow: Soft, forgiving snow that Makes even the clumsiest skier feel like a superstar. Cheers to looking good on the slopes!

Hoot and holler: The inevitable cheers, whoops, and shouts of joy echoing down the mountain after a perfect powder run.

Hot lap: The ultimate adrenaline rush: quickly skiing or snowboarding down a run and immediately going back up for another go. Repeat for maximum thrills!

Ice fall: A steep, frozen waterfall or ice-covered feature, offering a unique challenge for those seeking a technical descent.

Knee-deep: When your waist-deep in snow and every turn feels like you're floating on clouds. It's like a snow angel's dream come true!

Lap tracker: That one friend keeping count of how many runs the crew has done, as if the mountain was a scoreboard.

Lazy turns: Wide, slow, swooping turns in powder—perfect for soaking in the views and savoring every floaty second.

Line: The path you choose to take down the mountain. A well-thought-out line means more than just skiing—it's an art!

Over the head: Powder so deep, it engulfs you entirely on the way down. A good excuse for why your goggles are foggy!

Party lap: The ultimate encore—a carefree, good-times-only run where the only goal is to shred smiles and celebrate the day's powder party.

Phantom pole plant: Sticking your pole into powder only to find there's no resistance at all. It's like stabbing a ghost.

Pillaging the pow: When the group completely devours every flake of fresh snow on a slope, leaving it thoroughly shredded.

Pillow line: Who says skiing isn't playful? A pillow line lets you bounce down snowy cushions like a winter trampoline—graceful or not, it's pure fun.

Pillow pusher: A skier or rider who loves bouncing off every snow-covered ledge they can find, turning the mountain into their personal trampoline.

Pine needling: Watch your step! Pine needling is where nature's debris adds a dash of challenge to your powder day—sharp eyes and sharp turns required.

Plunge: The thrill of diving into a steep, powder-filled slope, feeling the adrenaline rush as you head downhill.

Pow: The affectionate nickname for powder snow. It's short, sweet, and gets your heart racing every time.

Powder frenzy: That wild energy in the cat when everyone sees untracked snow below. Cue the cheers and gear checks!

Powder limo: Another nickname for the snowcat. It's the height of backcountry luxury!

Powder pig: If your only goal is to chase and devour deep snow, you're a powder pig. No judgment—it's a badge of honor in the powder-obsessed world.

Powder pileup: When everyone scrambles out of the cat at once, tripping over one another in the rush to claim first tracks.

Powder poodle: A playful term for those who stick to the soft, easy stuff and steer clear of the gnarlier terrain. No judgment—they're living their fluffy dream.

Pucker factor: That heart-in-your-throat moment before dropping into a line that's just a bit outside your comfort zone.

Puke fest: When the snow is falling so heavily, it looks like the sky is "puking" snow. Gross name, but skiers love it!

Ridge line: The mountain's crown, where the adventure begins! Standing on the ridge line, you're gazing at a whole world of untouched snow below, your path ready to be carved. It's like the mountain is whispering, "This is your moment, go for it!" It's the perfect starting point for a thrilling descent—one that takes you into the heart of nature's snowy playground.

Rime: Nature's icy art! Rime decorates trees and rocks with frosty elegance, turning your skiing backdrop into a winter wonderland.

Ripper: A skier or snowboarder who just crushes the mountain, ripping through runs with confidence and style.

Rough and ready: Terrain that's challenging but rewarding, full of bumps, dips, and drops that make the skiing adventure extra exciting.

Runout: Your victory lap, a mellow glide after a steep thrill ride. It's where you high-five your crew and savor your snowy triumph.

Sastrugi: Wind-sculpted snow that looks cool but feels rough under your skis. Nature's art, but not the most fun to ride.

Secret stash: Treasure-hunt time! A stash is like finding buried gold—but it's fresh powder, hidden away from the crowds. Shred these secret spots for the ultimate ski bragging rights.

Send it!: The ultimate ski command. It means "go for it," whether it's a jump, a steep line, or just having the best day ever.

Shotgun start: Everyone racing to claim the best lines the second the cat door opens. A friendly (or not-) free-for-all.

Shotgun seat: The coveted front seat in the snowcat with the best view. Bagging this spot is a bragging right in itself!

Shred: It's not just a word; it's a vibe! When you're carving through the powder with pure speed and style, you're shredding like a pro.

Shredding the gnarr: Ripping through tough, gnarly terrain with confidence and skill. It's the ultimate phrase for those who attack the mountain head-on.

Ski bomb: A skier or snowboarder who charges hard and fast, often going full throttle down a powder-filled slope with reckless abandon.

Ski track: Every ski track is a story in the snow, leaving your mark as you carve through powdery slopes. Follow someone's path or create your own snowy signature!

Slay the dragon: Conquering a particularly gnarly line or intimidating slope. It's not just skiing—it's a quest!

Slope serenity: That feeling when you're gliding through untouched powder, surrounded by nothing but the peaceful silence of the backcountry. It's the calm before the thrilling ride.

Sluff: A small avalanche of loose snow that follows you as you ski down the mountain. It's your snowy sidekick, often trailing in your wake!

Snow angel recovery: That moment after a wipeout where you just lie there, arms and legs spread, enjoying the peace.

Snow bomb: The rush of powder that flies up after you hit the perfect jump or slope. It's like the snow's applause for your amazing descent!

Snowcap: The snowy peak that's a beacon for adventure, leading you to untouched runs and offering breathtaking views from the top.

Snow catapult: That unexpected launch when your skis or board hit a hidden snowdrift or pillow. Hold on tight and stick the landing.

Snow farm: A wide-open area where the snow just seems to grow in endless, dreamy blankets. A powder paradise waiting to be harvested!

Snow fatigue: When your legs scream for a break, but your powder-loving heart keeps saying, "Just one more run!"

Snow ghosts: These frosted trees, nicknamed "snow ghosts," haunt the mountains with their eerie beauty, standing watch over your powder adventures.

Snowpack: Think of snowpack as a mountain's mood ring. Layers of fluffy powder, icy crusts, and everything in between tell the story of the season. Each turn carves through this wintry diary.

Snow pillows: Soft, snow-packed mounds often formed around rocks or trees, perfect for a playful ride or a big jump.

Snow pit: It's like a snow scientist's lab, but cooler. A snow pit is a small hole you dig to examine the snow layers for avalanche risks. Think of it as the mountain's version of a doctor's checkup.

Spicy: Guide speak for hang on tight, things are going to get deliciously dicey

Steep and deep: When the snow is deep and the slope is steep, it's the ultimate cat skiing dream combo. A true test for thrill-seekers!

Stoke: The electric excitement you feel before, during, and after an epic day on the mountain. It's the thrill of fresh powder, the joy of carving perfect turns, and the laughs you share with your crew. Simply put, stoke is the energy that makes every ride unforgettable.

Straight flipping down: In K3, this phrase captures the essence of launching straight down a steep, untouched slope without hesitation—letting gravity do its thing. It's all about embracing the heart-pounding thrill of the descent and charging full speed into the rush of steep, untracked terrain.

Switchback: A series of turns or zigzags that take you up a steep slope. It's like a fun, winding road trip but on snow.

Sun crust: A sneaky snow layer baked hard by the sun, hiding under the fresh fluff. It's nature's crunchy surprise—tread (or shred) carefully!

Surf the white wave: Riding powder so deep and smooth it feels like catching waves on a tropical beach—minus the warmth.

Terrain Park: Nature's playground on steroids! Whether it's natural kickers or gnarly tree gaps, some cat skiing spots throw in wild features to keep you on your toes (or skis).

The back seat: When you lean too far back on your skis or board and end up flailing—or wiping out. Stay balanced, people!

Tight trees: For the bold and the brave, tight trees are forest sections with closely spaced trees, demanding precision as you weave through them in search of untouched powder.

Top-of-the-world stare: That collective pause at the summit as everyone silently marvels at the untouched beauty below. It's the calm before the powder storm.

Tree line: Hit the magical tree line, where the forest ends and wide-open alpine slopes begin. It's where the skiing feels limitless and the views take your breath away.

Tree well: A tree well might look innocent, but it's a hidden danger—a deep pocket of loose snow around a tree's base. Stay aware and steer wide.

Vertical drop: It's all downhill from here—in the best way possible. Vertical drop is your measure of glory, capturing the thrill of descending from mountaintop to base.

Whiskey turns: Super relaxed, wobbly turns—typically made after a celebratory swig from a hip flask at the top. Hey, it's après-ski somewhere!

White room: That magical moment when you're skiing through deep powder and the snow surrounds you like a soft, white cloud—everything is just a blur of white bliss.

Whoomph: The sound of settling snow beneath your skis or snowboard, often signaling a shift in snowpack stability—a warning from the mountain to stay alert.

Wind buff: When wind has smoothed out the snow on a run, making it feel buttery and fast—just the kind of surface you'll want to carve through.

Wind lip: The edge of a snowdrift or cornice where the wind has shaped the snow into a steep lip, often creating the perfect launch point for an exhilarating drop.

Yard sale: When you wipe out so spectacularly that your gear scatters everywhere, it's a yard sale. Bonus points if your goggles land in a tree.

PANTRY & PRODUCE

Great cooking starts with great ingredients. Buy the best you can within reason—flavor comes from quality, not perfection. Skip "light" or "low-fat" products when possible; they're often packed with fillers or sugar. Instead, choose ingredients that truly deliver, real butter, whole milk, and rich, full-bodied dairy that taste like something.

Keep oils simple. Everyday cooking calls for butter or olive oil. Save extra virgin olive oil for dressings, use coconut oil for baking or high-heat dishes, and reach for avocado oil when you want something mild and versatile.

The little touches make all the difference. Pure vanilla extract brings warmth and depth that artificial versions can't match, and natural maple syrup adds mellow sweetness. When it comes to meat, grass-fed, pasture-raised, or organic options are worth seeking out when available. Free-range or pasture-raised eggs have a richer flavor, and fresh, seasonal produce—especially from local markets—always tastes best while supporting your community. For the ingredients that really matter, organic is often worth the extra step.

Pantry staples deserve a little attention, too. Whole spices ground fresh are far more fragrant, unrefined or sea salts add lovely depth, and simple, additive-free dried fruits, beans, and grains form the backbone of countless great meals. With just a few high-quality basics, even the simplest dish can taste extraordinary.

Most of the recipes here work beautifully anywhere, though if you're cooking at higher elevations, you may need a few small tweaks—see *Altitude Adjustment: Cooking Above the Clouds* for tips.

Above all, I hope these recipes inspire you to cook, share, and connect. Food is more than ingredients—it's about gathering, sharing, and finding joy in the process. Don't aim for perfection; let your senses guide you. Cook with curiosity, savor the flavors, and enjoy every moment—because cooking should always be fun.

Happy cooking!

THANK YOU!

My first thanks go to Toni, my partner and alpine sidekick—without you, I never would have started this book.

A huge thank you to the incredible K3 staff—for lifting, hauling, and unloading deliveries, navigating snowmobiles through winter chaos, and making sure every perishable makes it safely to the lodge. Season after season, so many of you return, bringing not only your skills but also a true sense of community. Your energy, friendship, and unstoppable team spirit keep everything running smoothly, even when the unexpected happens. It's the people, as much as the place, that make K3 so special.

To David and Kris—for patiently answering my endless questions and helping me sort through the jumble of facts. To Tim—for your photos and your deep knowledge of K3's tenure and history, which gave so many recipes their roots. To Todd—for sharing stories and memories from K3's early days, adding both color and character to these pages. To Kristen—for your patience in shaping the cover and making it truly shine. And to Andi—for your camaraderie, your spätzle, and yes—I couldn't resist including your brownie recipe.

A heartfelt thank you to my friends and family for all your encouragement and support. To my brother and muse, Andy—your insight, your gift for keeping me grounded, and those much-needed reality checks made all the difference. To Mandy—for your advice, honesty, and wisdom that always steered me back on track. And to Sue—for the wine, the cheese, and the endless chats—thank you.

To the K3 guests—many of you have made your time at K3 your winter tradition. Your loyalty and love of good food and snow inspired me to write this book. We love hosting you, and I hope we'll see even more of you in the seasons to come.

And to Eddie, my design editor—for patiently reading my text and guiding me back on track. To Kelly—whose careful copyediting refined every recipe to perfection. To Liliana—whose eye for design placed each image perfectly and turned this book into something truly beautiful. And to Sara—the photographer who made every dish look as irresistible as it tastes.

Creating this book has been its own mountain to climb—thank you to everyone who helped me reach the summit. It's been one incredible journey, and I'm so grateful to have shared it with you.

ABOUT THE AUTHOR

I was born in London to Polish parents and grew up with a nomadic lifestyle. Thanks to my father's work, we were constantly on the move—and those early travels sparked a lifelong love of food from different cultures.

After finishing school, I went to culinary college, then completed my training in the fast-paced restaurant kitchens of London's West End. But it didn't take long for me to realize that being chained to a stove all day wasn't the kind of adventure I was looking for.

A ski season in the Alps opened my eyes to a different way of living—one that combined the outdoors, sport, and meaningful connections with people. A few months later, I found myself cooking aboard a yacht in the South of France. What was meant to be a single season turned into a twenty-year journey as a personal chef.

My career has taken me from dive boats in Australia to ski chalets in Switzerland and Austria, and aboard some of the most prestigious charter yachts in the world—often for high-profile and famous clients—across the Mediterranean and Caribbean. Along the way, I've discovered that food is so much more than sustenance. It's a way to connect, share stories, and bring people together—wherever you are in the world.

Traveling extensively has shaped my cooking style into an eclectic blend of classic techniques, contemporary flair, and global inspiration. I thrive on the unpredictability and adventure of it all. Every day brings something new, and I love having to improvise—drawing on local ingredients, adapting to unfamiliar environments, and connecting with people from all walks of life. Routine doesn't exist in my vocabulary—and that's exactly what keeps it exciting.

I met David through a mutual friend when he was looking for a chef to step in at his newly built South Park Lodge for the final weeks of its first season. It was a spontaneous request, but one unexpected email later, I booked a ticket, packed my knives, and headed to the mountains—unsure of what to expect but ready for whatever adventure awaited at the end of the road.

This was in March 2020, just before COVID hit, though none of us knew what was coming. While the world was shifting beneath our feet, I found myself at the lodge baking muffins, swapping stories with guests, and catching snippets of news that grew more surreal by the day. As the snow kept falling outside, everything else quietly began to unravel.

When I finished my stint and flew back to Spain, the world was a completely different place. Borders were closing, lockdowns were looming, and the lodge felt like a dream I'd just woken up from. The following season, Canada was shut tight—I couldn't return. But the year after that, I was back at the lodge, and I've returned every season since, spending most of the winter up in those mountains, doing what I love in a place that feels like home.

For this book, I've turned my creative focus to the warmth and rustic style of lodge cooking—soul-satisfying recipes made for snowy days. Every recipe has been cooked countless times at the lodge, often requested, and well loved by our returning guests. Over the years, many dishes have evolved, subtly shaped by preferences and feedback. This book is a tribute to the comfort, connection, and joy found in sharing a meal after a day in the mountains.

PHOTO CREDITS

Ski Journal Magazine: Front cover, pp. 4, 6-7, 19, 20-21, 32-33, 44-45, 60, 85, 94, 111, 118, 123, 140-141, 148-149, 165

Steve Smith/Shutterstock: Pp. 10-11

Kris Moore: Pp. 16-17

Sara Savage: Pp. 26, 51, 59, 69, 89, 92, 97, 125, 122-123, 137

Toni Martin Avila: Back cover, pp. 48, 103

Guajillo Studios/Shutterstock: Pp. 52

Zoya Lynch: Pp. 62-63, 74-75, 86-87, 104-105, 116-117, 154-155

Tatjana Baibakova/Shutterstock: Pp 126

Tim Mc Allister: Pp. 151

Ewa Lubienski: Pp 160

Pundapanda/Shutterstock: Pp 170

David Moore: Pp 173

Sofia Winghamre: Pp174

Copyright © 2025 by Ewa Lubienski

All rights reserved. No part of this book may be reproduced or used in any manner without written permission of the copyright owner except for the use of quotations in a book review.

For more information, contact: ewalubienski@gmail.com

First edition 2025

Development editing by Edie Jarolim
Book interior design by Liliana Guia
Cover design by Kristen Meilicke
Copy editing by Kelly Messier

ISBN 978-1-9193088-0-7
Ebook ISBN 978-1-9193088-1-4

www.ewalubienski.com

www.ingramcontent.com/pod-product-compliance
Lightning Source LLC
Chambersburg PA
CBHW040046100526
44584CB00034BA/4459